04-07-2004

GHj

HENRY
AARON

HENRY AARON

Richard Scott Rennert

CHELSEA HOUSE PUBLISHERS
New York   Philadelphia

Chelsea House Publishers
Editor-in-Chief Richard S. Papale
Executive Managing Editor Karyn Gullen Browne
Copy Chief Philip Koslow
Picture Editor Adrian G. Allen
Art Director Nora Wertz
Manufacturing Director Gerald Levine
Systems Manager Lindsey Ottman
Production Coordinator Marie Claire Cebrián-Ume

Black Americans of Achievement
Senior Editor Richard Rennert

Staff for HENRY AARON
Copy Editor Danielle Janusz
Editorial Assistant Nicole Greenblatt
Designer Diana Blume
Picture Researcher Alan Gottlieb
Cover Illustration Dan O'Leary

3 5 7 9 8 6 4 2

Library of Congress Cataloging-in-Publication Data
Rennert, Richard Scott, 1956–
    Henry Aaron, baseball great/Richard Scott Rennert
      p. cm.—(Black Americans of achievement)
    Includes bibliographical references and index.
  ISBN 0-7910-1859-8
         0-7910-1888-1(pbk.)
  1. Aaron, Hank, 1934–. 2. Baseball players—United
States—Biography—. I. Title. II. Series.
GV865.A25S35 1993
796.357'092—dc20   92-17156
[B]   CIP

To Rozelle from Milwaukee

Frontispiece: *Henry Aaron assumes
his picture-perfect batting stance in
1963, the year he won the second
of his four National League home
run titles. He also led the league
in homers in 1957, 1966, and
1967.*

CONTENTS

BLACK AMERICANS OF ACHIEVEMENT

HENRY AARON
baseball great

KAREEM ABDUL-JABBAR
basketball great

RALPH ABERNATHY
civil rights leader

ALVIN AILEY
choreographer

MUHAMMAD ALI
heavyweight champion

RICHARD ALLEN
religious leader and social activist

MAYA ANGELOU
author

LOUIS ARMSTRONG
musician

ARTHUR ASHE
tennis great

JOSEPHINE BAKER
entertainer

JAMES BALDWIN
author

BENJAMIN BANNEKER
scientist and mathematician

AMIRI BARAKA
poet and playwright

COUNT BASIE
bandleader and composer

ROMARE BEARDEN
artist

JAMES BECKWOURTH
frontiersman

MARY MCLEOD BETHUNE
educator

JULIAN BOND
civil rights leader and politician

GWENDOLYN BROOKS
poet

JIM BROWN
football great

BLANCHE BRUCE
politician

RALPH BUNCHE
diplomat

STOKELY CARMICHAEL
civil rights leader

GEORGE WASHINGTON CARVER
botanist

RAY CHARLES
musician

CHARLES CHESNUTT
author

JOHN COLTRANE
musician

BILL COSBY
entertainer

PAUL CUFFE
merchant and abolitionist

COUNTEE CULLEN
poet

BENJAMIN DAVIS, SR., AND BENJAMIN DAVIS, JR.
military leaders

SAMMY DAVIS, JR.
entertainer

FATHER DIVINE
religious leader

FREDERICK DOUGLASS
abolitionist editor

CHARLES DREW
physician

W. E. B. DU BOIS
scholar and activist

PAUL LAURENCE DUNBAR
poet

KATHERINE DUNHAM
dancer and choreographer

DUKE ELLINGTON
bandleader and composer

RALPH ELLISON
author

JULIUS ERVING
basketball great

JAMES FARMER
civil rights leader

ELLA FITZGERALD
singer

MARCUS GARVEY
black nationalist leader

JOSH GIBSON
baseball great

DIZZY GILLESPIE
musician

ALEX HAILEY
author

PRINCE HALL
social reformer

WILLIAM HASTIE
educator and politician

MATTHEW HENSON
explorer

CHESTER HIMES
author

BILLIE HOLIDAY
singer

JOHN HOPE
educator

LENA HORNE
entertainer

LANGSTON HUGHES
poet

ZORA NEALE HURSTON
author

JESSE JACKSON
civil rights leader and politician

MICHAEL JACKSON
entertainer

JACK JOHNSON
heavyweight champion

JAMES WELDON JOHNSON
author

MAGIC JOHNSON
basketball great

SCOTT JOPLIN
composer

BARBARA JORDAN
politician

CORETTA SCOTT KING
civil rights leader

MARTIN LUTHER KING, JR.
civil rights leader

LEWIS LATIMER
scientist

SPIKE LEE
filmmaker

REGINALD LEWIS
entrepreneur

ALAIN LOCKE
scholar and educator

JOE LOUIS
heavyweight champion

RONALD MCNAIR
astronaut

MALCOLM X
militant black leader

THURGOOD MARSHALL
Supreme Court justice

TONI MORRISON
author

CONSTANCE BAKER
MOTLEY
*civil rights leader
and judge*

ELIJAH MUHAMMAD
religious leader

EDDIE MURPHY
entertainer

JESSE OWENS
champion athlete

SATCHEL PAIGE
baseball great

CHARLIE PARKER
musician

GORDON PARKS
photographer

ROSA PARKS
civil rights leader

SIDNEY POITIER
actor

ADAM CLAYTON
POWELL, JR.
political leader

COLIN POWELL
military leader

LEONTYNE PRICE
opera singer

A. PHILIP RANDOLPH
labor leader

PAUL ROBESON
singer and actor

JACKIE ROBINSON
baseball great

DIANA ROSS
entertainer

BILL RUSSELL
basketball great

JOHN RUSSWURM
publisher

SOJOURNER TRUTH
antislavery activist

HARRIET TUBMAN
antislavery activist

NAT TURNER
slave revolt leader

DENMARK VESEY
slave revolt leader

ALICE WALKER
author

MADAM C. J. WALKER
entrepreneur

BOOKER T. WASHINGTON
educator and racial spokesman

IDA WELLS-BARNETT
civil rights leader

WALTER WHITE
civil rights leader

OPRAH WINFREY
entertainer

STEVIE WONDER
musician

RICHARD WRIGHT
author

ON
ACHIEVEMENT
————— ❧ —————

Coretta Scott King

Bᴇꜰᴏʀᴇ ʏᴏᴜ ʙᴇɢɪɴ this book, I hope you will ask yourself what the word *excellence* means to you. I think that it's a question we should all ask, and keep asking as we grow older and change. Because the truest answer to it should never change. When you think of excellence, perhaps you think of success at work; or of becoming wealthy; or meeting the right person, getting married, and having a good family life.

Those important goals are worth striving for, but there is a better way to look at excellence. As Martin Luther King, Jr., said in one of his last sermons, "I want you to be first in love. I want you to be first in moral excellence. I want you to be first in generosity. If you want to be important, wonderful. If you want to be great, wonderful. But recognize that he who is greatest among you shall be your servant."

My husband, Martin Luther King, Jr., knew that the true meaning of achievement is service. When I met him, in 1952, he was already ordained as a Baptist preacher and was working toward a doctoral degree at Boston University. I was studying at the New England Conservatory and dreamed of accomplishments in music. We married a year later, and after I graduated the following year we moved to Montgomery, Alabama. We didn't know it then, but our notions of achievement were about to undergo a dramatic change.

You may have read or heard about what happened next. What began with the boycott of a local bus line grew into a national movement, and by the time he was assassinated in 1968 my husband had fashioned a black movement powerful enough to shatter forever the practice of racial segregation. What you may not have read about is where he got his method for resisting injustice without compromising his religious beliefs.

He adopted the strategy of nonviolence from a man of a different race, who lived in a different country, and even practiced a different religion. The man was Mahatma Gandhi, the great leader of India, who devoted his life to serving humanity in the spirit of love and nonviolence. It was in these principles that Martin discovered his method for social reform. More than anything else, those two principles were the key to his achievements.

This book is about black Americans who served society through the excellence of their achievements. It forms a part of the rich history of black men and women in America—a history of stunning accomplishments in every field of human endeavor, from literature and art to science, industry, education, diplomacy, athletics, jurisprudence, even polar exploration.

Not all of the people in this history had the same ideals, but I think you will find something that all of them had in common. Like Martin Luther King, Jr., they all decided to become "drum majors" and serve humanity. In that principle—whether it was expressed in books, inventions, or song—they found something outside themselves to use as a goal and a guide. Something that showed them a way to serve others, instead of only living for themselves.

Reading the stories of these courageous men and women not only helps us discover the principles that we will use to guide our own lives but also teaches us about our black heritage and about America itself. It is crucial for us to know the heroes and heroines of our history and to realize that the price we paid in our struggle for equality in America was dear. But we must also understand that we have gotten as far as we have partly because America's democratic system and ideals made it possible.

We are still struggling with racism and prejudice. But the great men and women in this series are a tribute to the spirit of our democratic ideals and the system in which they have flourished. And that makes their stories special and worth knowing. ❧

1

"HAMMER OUT
A LITTLE JUSTICE"

⬤

T HE SUN HAD just come up on February 27, 1958, when Henry Aaron finished putting his baseball gear into the trunk of his new Chevrolet Malibu and got behind the steering wheel. The 24-year-old ballplayer had always arrived on time for the opening of the Milwaukee Braves' spring training camp. And he had no intention of setting a bad example now that he had established himself, after four seasons with the ballclub, as one of the National League's brightest stars.

Waving good-bye to his wife and in-laws, Aaron swung his car into the Jacksonville traffic and drove across the city to pick up teammate Felix Mantilla, who had also been visiting relatives in Florida. The two major leaguers then started the five-hour drive to Bradenton, the Braves' spring training site on the Sunshine State's Gulf Coast. The day had arrived to get ready for the upcoming baseball season after nearly five full months of fanfare, family, and fun.

The revelry had begun on October 10, 1957, the instant Milwaukee had recorded the final out against the heavily favored New York Yankees in the seventh game of the World Series. The events immediately surrounding the celebration of the Braves' first World Series triumph in 43 years remained a blur in Aaron's memory. But he had little trouble recalling the

A moment in Henry Aaron's "shiningest hour" with the Milwaukee Braves: teammate Johnny Logan showers the 23-year-old with champagne following his 11th-inning, pennant-winning home run on September 23, 1957. That year, Aaron noted, "there was plenty to celebrate—namely, the world championship, the MVP award, our new home, and most of all, our growing family."

Milwaukee County Stadium is jammed with baseball rooters on October 5, 1957, as the first World Series game ever played in the home of the Milwaukee Braves gets under way. "The people of Wisconsin," Aaron said later, "were the warmest, friendliest fans in the world. . . . Any player would have been fortunate to play in front of those fans."

heroes' welcome he and his teammates received from their adoring fans upon returning to Milwaukee from New York. "Those people were out of their minds," he remembered in *"Aaron, r.f.,"* his first autobiography. "We got involved in the damnedest parade you ever saw, from the airport into town, and around town, and it seemed like it would never end."

When the Braves moved their franchise to Wisconsin from Boston five years earlier, Milwaukee earned the distinction of being the smallest city in the nation to have a big league team. Yet there was nothing small-time about baseball rooters in the Midwest. They flocked to Milwaukee County Stadium from Iowa, Minnesota, North Dakota, and South Dakota, as well as from every rural town in Wisconsin, establishing a National League attendance record in the club's first season there. These midwesterners were so delighted to have major league baseball in their part of the country they cheered wildly even for foul balls.

Milwaukee became the undisputed baseball capital of America in the four campaigns that followed. Each year, the Braves became the first of the 16 big league franchises to reach the 1 million mark in attendance. And when Milwaukee vaulted to the top of the National League standings in 1957, the Midwest's excitement over baseball peaked: the ball-club drew 2.2 million fans, setting an all-time major league attendance record.

During that magic summer of 1957, future Hall of Famers Eddie Mathews, Albert ("Red") Schoen-dienst, and Warren Spahn were among the Braves players who became as revered as conquering warriors returning from a battlefield. But no one on the squad was more highly prized than Aaron, whose masterful performance in the World Series mirrored his brilliant all-around play during the regular season. Shortly after the World Series ended, he was named the National League's most valuable player for 1957.

The rewards continued to pile up as Aaron traveled to his Alabama hometown after the season. He arrived in Mobile on the Hummingbird, the fanciest train on the Louisville & Nashville line. At the city's railroad station, a brass band played "Take Me Out to the Ballgame" and "On Mobile Bay" as 2,000 well-wishers cheered their returning hero. Mayor Joseph Langan handed him the key to the city and declared that Hank Aaron Day would commence the following morning. The city helped Aaron celebrate his big day by giving him a huge parade through the streets of Mobile. Joining the procession of marching bands and floats, he waved to the crowds from the backseat of a convertible.

"If there was ever a time I felt like crying for joy, just plain old happiness," Aaron said, "that was it." He was the top player in the National League and a World Series star. He had been given a hefty salary raise to around $40,000—making him one of the highest-paid players on the team—and the key to his hometown. He had bought a roomy new house in Mequon, a suburb north of Milwaukee, and he had a beautiful three-year-old daughter, Gaile. In addition, his wife, Barbara, had given birth to their first son,

Aaron returns to his Alabama hometown for a hero's welcome on October 25, 1957, with his first wife, Barbara, and seven-month-old son, Hankie. "When we made the trip to Mobile after the World Series in 1957," he recalled, "we did it in style for a change, arriving on the L&N Hummingbird. Mobile had arranged a Hank Aaron Day, and I decided the only proper way to get there was aboard the Hummingbird, which to me was like leaving town in an old beat-up Volkswagen and returning in a Rolls-Royce."

Hankie, at the start of the year and to twins, Gary and Lary, in December. (Born prematurely, Gary never made it out of the hospital; but Lary was brought to Mobile and thrived under the constant care of his paternal grandmother.)

For Henry Aaron, motoring down the Gulf Coast in early 1958, life could hardly be sweeter—or so it would seem. Yet his glory-filled world was far from perfect. The specter of racism lurked at each bend of the road to Bradenton.

In 1958, little more than a decade after Jackie Robinson had broken major league baseball's color barrier, Bradenton, like most southern towns, was still racially segregated. Local statutes barred blacks from the better-equipped white schools and hospitals and required them to use separate restaurants, drinking fountains, and seating sections at movie theaters and the ballpark. Aaron recalled in *I Had a Hammer*, his most recent autobiography, that the racial discrimination was so pronounced "some of the newspapers in Florida wouldn't even print pictures of the black players."

In Aaron's previous four visits to Bradenton, his skin color had prevented him from staying at the Manatee River Hotel, where his white teammates roomed. He had always lodged instead with schoolteacher Lulu Gibson and her husband, a black couple who owned a modest home on the black side of town. At the rear of the Gibsons' property stood a garage with two small upstairs rooms, and through 1956 Aaron had shared these cramped quarters with several black teammates. When he had returned to Bradenton in early 1957 as the reigning National League batting champion, the Gibsons had invited him to stay in the "big house," and he was hoping the Most Valuable Player Award would merit a similar invitation in 1958.

Aaron and Mantilla were still on the highway to Bradenton, not far from the town limits, when a big Buick came up behind their car and began butting against the Chevrolet's rear bumper. Thinking the driver wanted to pass him, Aaron pulled onto the roadway's shoulder to let the Buick go ahead. As the vehicle sped by, he saw a gang of white teenagers inside.

But the Buick did not continue along the highway. Instead, it slowed to a crawl, waiting to resume its dangerous game with the Chevrolet. Aaron shot past the big sedan, whereupon the Buick rushed up from behind once again. This time, rather than tap his front fender against the Chevrolet's bumper, the Buick's driver steered his automobile into the adjoining lane.

Aaron could hear the carload of white youths accelerate. Then he saw it veer sharply. "They ripped into the front of my car at sixty miles an hour," he recalled. "Felix and I went into a ditch, then bounced out and swerved into the highway, with cars speeding all around us." Remarkably, both ballplayers managed to avoid serious injury.

Aaron discussed the incident with a few newspapermen as soon as he reached the Braves' training camp. A couple of articles about the attempt on his life were printed; but for the most part his story fell on deaf ears. In 1958, the civil rights movement was still in its infancy, and the voice of a lone black man carried little authority—even when the voice belonged to a three-time major league all-star.

Henry Aaron understood that if he wanted people to listen to him "hammer out a little justice," he was going to have to do much more than make the all-star team every year. He would have to establish himself as one of the greatest baseball players of all time. ❧

During the first half-dozen spring trainings that Aaron attended in Bradenton, Florida, local statutes barred blacks from lodging at the same facilities as whites. "The white players stayed at the big, pink Manatee River Hotel," he remembered, "and the black players lived in an apartment over a garage owned by a black schoolteacher named Lulu Gibson [pictured at right]. That is, most of us lived in the apartment—the penthouse, as we called it. . . . The elder statesman among us . . . had 'big house' privileges, which meant he had a room in the main house."

2
"CRAZY ABOUT BASEBALL"

H ENRY AARON WAS, above all, a child of the South. He was born on February 5, 1934, in Down the Bay, the section of Mobile, Alabama, where poor blacks resided. To young Henry, the black side of his hometown was, if not exactly a boy's paradise, then a pleasant enough place in which to grow up. Surrounded by a loving family and friendly neighbors, he stayed out of trouble and went to school, read sports books, helped with the household chores, and—his favorite activity of all—played ball. From the first time he took a broom handle and used it to swat bottle caps around his front yard, Henry was, as he put it in *I Had a Hammer*, "crazy about baseball."

Herbert Aaron, Henry's father, loved the sport, too. At one point, he even started a baseball team through the small tavern he ran; Henry would ac-

The future home run king was born in a ramshackle house on this street in Mobile, Alabama, and lived there for eight years, until he moved with his family to the nearby hamlet of Toulminville in 1942. "It was in Toulminville that I became a ballplayer," Aaron recalled. "There were open spaces in Toulminville, and before long, enough kids had moved in that we could generally get up a game."

company his father to the local games and peddle cold drinks to the crowd. Unfortunately, the demands of supporting a family in the throes of the Great Depression prevented the senior Aaron from taking the field very often. Whenever there were enough jobs to go around, he worked as a boilermaker's assistant at the Alabama Drydock and Shipbuilding Company.

During Henry's early years, the depression periodically forced his father to be laid off from work. Yet Herbert Aaron and his wife, Estella, found that life in Mobile, Alabama's only seaport, was a step up from the lowly sharecroppers' existence they had endured in Camden, a farming community 125 miles to the north. Herbert hailed from a line of preachers, but he had no interest in spending his days as a man of the cloth, let alone a cotton picker. Shortly after he married, he departed for Mobile, a city of nearly 80,000.

As soon as Herbert settled in Down the Bay, he sent for his wife. There they lived in a small residence that they rented for nine dollars a month. It was in this home, at 666 Wilkinson, that Henry and his elder siblings, Herbert, Jr., and Sarah, were born.

"I was a mama's boy," Henry admitted in *"Aaron, r.f."* Even though he was not the baby of the family—Tommie, Alfred, Alfreda, Gloria, and James were born after him—he always received a great deal of attention from his mother. "I never knew problems or tensions," Henry said of his childhood. "It was just normal, everyday, average, Negro American family life."

As the house began to fill up, Henry's father decided to move his growing clan to Toulminville, a hamlet just beyond the Mobile city limits. In 1942, right after Henry turned eight, Herbert Aaron purchased two small lots on a fairly empty stretch of road for about $100. With the help of Henry and the other children, Herbert collected the leftover lumber from a nearby home that had recently been razed. Then he hired a pair of carpenters to construct a modest six-room, wood-frame house at 2010 Edwards Street, the family's new address in Toulminville.

"There were no lights in our house," Henry remembered in *I Had a Hammer*, "not even windows. A kerosene lamp was all we needed. The bathroom was an outhouse in the backyard. It was a good outhouse—we built it ourselves."

No one in the family had his or her own bed. Nor was the kitchen pantry ever stocked with store-bought food; the dinner fare consisted mostly of homegrown beans and greens and skillet-fried corn bread. To save money, Henry even used homemade baseballs; he made them by wrapping rags or nylon hose around old golf balls.

The Aarons never complained about these hard-ships because they did not think of themselves as being poor. "Everybody else was in the same boat," Henry recalled. "We didn't know to feel sorry for ourselves."

Henry, in fact, delighted in the move to Toul-minville. "There was," he said, "no better place to play ball." Because Toulminville attracted many other families and boasted acres of open fields, the budding athlete never lacked for playmates or a place to play.

At first, Henry and his friends held their games on a baseball diamond they laid out in an old pecan grove across the street from his house. (After Toul-minville officially became part of Mobile in 1945, the city turned the diamond and the surrounding land into Carver Park, a recreational area that featured regulation baseball fields.) If no one was around to start up a game or play catch, Henry would head back home and practice by himself. He sometimes spent

Moses Fleetwood Walker joined the Northwestern League's Toledo Blue Stockings as a catcher in 1883 and became baseball's first black big leaguer the following year, when the team moved up to the American Association. Dozens of other black ball-players—including Frank Grant, George Stovey, and Walker's brother, Weldy—followed Fleet's example and competed against white professionals through the late 1890s, before all blacks were barred from the major and minor leagues for the next half century.

MOORE   N.BELL   HAWKINS   DUNCAN   C.BELL   MOTHELL   McCALL   DRAKE   SWERTT   WILKINSON   DR.SMITH SPEDDEN

The members of the Pennsylvania-based Hilldale Club (opposite page), winners of the Eastern Colored League championship, line up at Kansas City's Muelebach Field on October 11, 1924, before meeting the Kansas City Monarchs (above), champions of the Negro National League, in the first modern Negro World Series. While Aaron was growing up, the poorly financed Negro leagues offered blacks their only opportunity to play organized professional baseball.

hours tossing a baseball onto the roof and hitting it with a stick or nabbing the ball with his mitt as it came tumbling down. He eventually got so good at these games that he would throw the baseball completely over the roof, race around the house, and catch the ball before it struck the ground.

A much more remarkable sight was Henry's batting style. For one thing, he swung with his weight on his front foot instead of his back foot and would lash out at the ball at the last possible moment. Even more unusual, he hit cross-handed, keeping his right hand closest to the knob of the bat. No one told him his technique was incorrect, that the proper way for a right-handed hitter to hold the bat was with the right hand above the left.

Sometimes Henry would go to Hartwell Field, take his seat in the ballpark's blacks-only section, and root for the Mobile Bears of the Southern Association. Watching these minor leaguers take their swings, he would notice that all the players, like his schoolboy friends, gripped the bat the opposite way he did. Yet he found it easy to hit cross-handed and saw no reason to alter his swing.

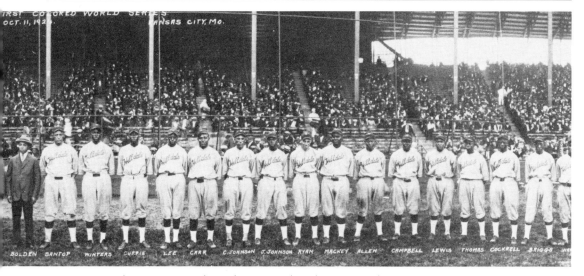

FIRST COLORED WORLD SERIES
OCT. 11, 192   KANSAS CITY, MO.

BOLDEN SANTOP   WINTERS CURRIS   LEE CARR   C.JOHNSON J.JOHNSON RYAN MACKEY ALLEN CAMPBELL LEWIS THOMAS COCKRELL BRIGGS

As much as Henry loved to catch, throw, and
bat, he knew better than to entertain dreams of
baseball glory. The first time he told his father he
planned to be in the big leagues, Herbert Aaron said
pointedly to his son, "Ain't no colored ballplayers."
Henry got the message. As much as he loved the
sport, he understood he could not count on following
in the footsteps of his boyhood idol, New York
Yankees center fielder Joe DiMaggio, because the
major leagues admitted white ballplayers only. Blacks
who wanted to play professional baseball in the early
1940s could do so solely in the racially segregated
Negro leagues.

Negro baseball dates back to at least 1867, when
two black ballclubs, the Brooklyn Uniques and the
Philadelphia Excelsiors, squared off against one
another on an October afternoon in Brooklyn. John
W. ("Bud") Fowler became the first black professional
ballplayer roughly five years later, when a white team
in Pennsylvania paid him to join their roster. Besides
Fowler, more than 60 blacks played on white baseball
teams before segregation laws were enforced at the
end of the 19th century.

Mobile's Central High School principal Dr. Benjamin Baker unwittingly encouraged Aaron to concentrate on playing baseball by having several run-ins with the teenager and souring him on school. Aaron recalled that in spite of his dreams of major league stardom, "until I was a teenager—and even then, up to a point—most of the organized ball I played was softball."

The first black to follow Fowler's lead into the professional ranks was Moses Fleetwood Walker. In 1884, Walker suited up for the Toledo Blue Stockings in the American Association (one of the earliest major leagues) 63 years before Jackie Robinson played in his first National League game. Meanwhile, scores of other black ballplayers launched their professional careers in the 1880s, but as members of independent teams, among them the Philadelphia Orions and the Long Island–based Cuban Giants.

Blacks were pretty much limited to playing on independent teams in each of the next three decades. Then, on February 13, 1920, in Kansas City, Missouri, Andrew ("Rube") Foster, formerly a star pitcher for such independent clubs as the Cuban X-Giants, Philadelphia Giants, and Waco Yellow Jackets, changed the course of black baseball by organizing the nation's first all-black league, the Negro National League. It consisted of eight teams: the Chicago American Giants, the Chicago Giants, the Cuban Stars, the Dayton Marcos, the Detroit Stars, the Indianapolis ABC's, the Kansas City Monarchs, and the St. Louis Giants. Three years later, the Eastern Colored League was formed; and in 1924, the first modern Negro World Series was held.

Many more black teams and leagues were founded over the next two decades, as organized black baseball, like the white major leagues, proceeded to grow in popularity. As Henry entered his teens, some of the ballclubs in the Negro leagues were drawing more than 10,000 spectators a game. Mobile had its own black club, the Black Bears, and they played at Mitchell Field.

Surprisingly, Henry never took part in an organized baseball game until he was well into his teens. Neither his elementary school, Toulminville Grammar School, nor his high school, Central High, fielded a team; nor did Mobile have a Little League he could join. During most of his youth, his lone opportunity to play baseball was in the pickup games at Carver Park.

On rare occasions, a few white players would take part in the games. These contests were held, Henry remembered, "off the beaten path where the police couldn't see us." Most of the time, however, the games remained segregated. In Mobile, the two races had little to do with one another except when blacks were employed by whites.

Henry's initial encounter with organized ball was in the all-black, fast-pitch softball league sponsored by the city's recreation department. He started out as a catcher, then became a pitcher and, finally, an infielder. The team he played for was named, fittingly enough, the Braves.

Away from the baseball diamond, Henry was just as attentive a student. "Education was always very important in our house," he recalled. "Mama ranked it right behind family and church." But he abruptly lost his enthusiasm for school when Jackie Robinson broke baseball's color barrier in 1947. Thrilled that the major leagues were no longer barring blacks, Henry believed it was only a matter of time before he would begin his own big league career.

Every April, as spring training drew to a close, a couple of the major league teams stopped at Mobile to play an exhibition game, then continued north to open the baseball season. In 1948, the Brooklyn Dodgers came to town, and no one was more excited over their arrival than 14-year-old Henry Aaron. When it was announced that Jackie Robinson would speak to the local black community in an auditorium on Davis Avenue, Henry skipped school so he could listen to his hero's address. The experience of seeing Robinson in person prompted the teenager to announce to his father that he would be in the majors by the time Robinson retired.

Henry did everything he could to make sure that nothing interfered with his plans. In addition to excelling at baseball, he was an outstanding football lineman, and his play on the Central High School team earned him a berth on the all-city squad. Henry worried, though, that he was ruining his prospects for a baseball career by playing football. He figured a college might offer him a football scholarship (which he knew his mother would never let him turn down), or he might suffer a serious injury on the gridiron. If either of these two things happened, he would be forced to give up baseball.

After thinking the matter over, the high school sophomore decided to quit the football team. "The principal at Central High, Dr. Benjamin Baker, took exception to my decision," Henry remembered, "and we got into a little argument over it. He ended up chasing me down the hall, waving his cane at me." Their heated exchange only soured Henry on Central High even more.

When the following spring arrived, Henry made it a point to cut out of school every afternoon the Dodgers had a ballgame. He would head for Davis Avenue and enter a pool hall that had a radio carrying a live broadcast of the game, and for the rest of the afternoon he would listen intently to the action. In this fashion, he managed to keep close track of Robinson's exploits for more than a month.

Inevitably, Baker caught up with the wayward student and expelled him from school. Henry was too terrified to tell his parents about his dismissal, so he pretended that nothing had happened. At the beginning of each school day, he made his way to Central High, strode up to the front entrance, walked straight through the building, and exited by a rear door. Then he went directly to the pool hall.

One day in the pool hall, Henry was astonished to see his father standing in the doorway. Herbert

Jackie Robinson, the National League's reigning most valuable player, signs his 1950 Brooklyn Dodgers contract under the watchful eye of Branch Rickey, the architect of baseball's integration experiment. Robinson, said Aaron, "always made it a point to get to know new black players as they came into the league and to make them realize they had a responsibility that went beyond playing ball. He made a special point of talking to the players he thought would be stars, because he knew that their voices would be heard over the others'. I was honored that he pulled me aside a few times."

Aaron motioned to his son to follow him home. Once there, they sat side by side in an old car parked in front of the house and had a long talk. Henry tried to explain that he was planning to become a ballplayer, and that he stood a better chance of learning how to be a success like Jackie Robinson if he spent his time listening to ballgames on the radio instead of sitting in a classroom. The senior Aaron did not object to Henry's dreams of stardom; he insisted only that his son get an education first.

"He said," Henry recalled, "that every morning he put two quarters in my pocket so I could go to school and have a good lunch, and he only took one quarter with him to work, because my education was more important than his stomach." As far as the problems at school were concerned, Herbert Aaron promised Henry he would not have to go back to Central High in the fall. He would be enrolled instead at a private school, the Josephine Allen Institute.

That summer, before the new school year started, Henry again spent most of his free time playing ball in Carver Park. He noticed during a recreation-league softball game that his every move at third base and at the plate was being studied by a man standing near one of the coach's boxes. Eventually, the man came forward and introduced himself: he was Ed Scott, manager of the Mobile Black Bears, and he wanted Henry to join their ballclub.

Even though Henry was flattered by the offer, he turned it down because the Black Bears held their home games on Sundays. In the Aaron household, that day of the week was reserved for church and family. Estella Aaron would never let him spend his Sundays playing ball with a bunch of grown men.

Scott, however, refused to take no for an answer. A former Negro league player with the Norfolk Stars, he was an excellent judge of talent, and he thought 16-year-old Henry was too good a ballplayer to let get away. Scott recalled years later that "my wife asked me why I just didn't leave those people alone. But I kept going by there." Every weekend, he would show up at 2010 Edwards Street and try to cajole Henry's mother into letting her son join the Black Bears.

The teenager, meanwhile, wanted no part of the discussions. He did not even want his mother to think he had anything to do with Scott's coming to their home. Whenever Henry saw Scott's car drive up the block, he hid behind the house until the Black Bears' manager had left.

After nearly a month of pleading, Scott finally won out. For $10 a game, which was a sizable amount of money for a high school student in 1950, Henry became a Black Bear. "He was green as he could be,"

Scott remembered. "He stood up there at the plate upright, no crouch at all, and the other team figured he wasn't ready. The pitcher tried to get a fastball by him, and he hit a line drive that banged against the old tin fence they had around the outfield out there—nearly put the ball through the fence. They walked him the rest of the time."

As promised, Henry entered the Josephine Allen Institute that fall, and he resumed playing for the Black Bears the following spring. He picked up right where he left off, hitting the ball with such authority that Scott phoned his friend McKinley ("Bunny") Downs, business manager of the Negro American League's Indianapolis Clowns, and insisted he come to Mobile and take a look at a budding star. Intrigued, Downs brought the Clowns south in mid-1951 for an exhibition game at Mitchell Field.

Henry did not disappoint his newest observer. Like a seasoned veteran, he stroked three base hits and handled each chance flawlessly at shortstop. After the game, Downs approached Henry.

"How old are you, kid?" the Clowns' business manager asked.

"Seventeen," Henry said.

"Are you still in high school?"

"Yessir."

"When do you get out?"

"I'll graduate next year."

"Do you always play shortstop?"

"I play anywhere they want me to play," Henry replied.

"That's a nice attitude. How would you like to play for the Indianapolis Clowns?"

"I don't see no reason why not," Henry told Downs.

But, as always, Estella Aaron had the last word in the matter. She made it clear to Downs that her son could not play in Indianapolis until he graduated

Ed Scott, a former Negro leagues ballplayer, was managing the Mobile Black Bears in 1940 when he spotted Aaron playing third base in a pickup game and convinced him to join the local black semipro team. "If I had waited in Mobile for a white baseball scout to find me," Aaron said later, "I don't know if I'd ever have been discovered for the big leagues or not."

from high school in June 1952. Downs said he understood, and that he would send Henry a contract the following year. "I figured," Henry said later, "I'd never hear from him again."

Meanwhile, the teenager's spirits were lifted by an announcement that the Brooklyn Dodgers organization would be holding a tryout camp in Mobile. The camp, which took place late in the summer of 1951, attracted every top ballplayer in the city; and for Mobile, that was saying a lot. Ever since LeRoy ("Satchel") Paige began his fabled career by pitching for the Mobile Tigers in the early 1920s, the city had been known as a breeding ground for superior baseball talent. In time, Henry would add to the luster of Mobile's reputation, as would his contemporaries Willie McCovey and Billy Williams; such younger stars as Tommie Agee, Cleon Jones, and Amos Otis; and even one of Henry's younger brothers, Tommie.

Unfortunately for Henry, the large number of talented ballplayers in Mobile made it easy for him to get lost in the shuffle. No sooner had he stepped into the batter's box at the tryout than he was chased away from the plate by an older player from Down the Bay. The same thing happened when Henry took the field to play shortstop. Because he hardly looked like a big leaguer—he stood less than six feet tall and weighed about 150 pounds—none of the officials who ran the camp thought to give him a second look. "One of the Dodger scouts told me I was too small," Henry remembered, "and that was it."

Bunny Downs, however, had not forgotten about the Black Bears' shortstop. Shortly after Henry's 18th birthday, the Clowns sent him a contract to play ball for $200 a month. It was too much money to turn down, even though signing the contract would mean having to report for spring training before Henry graduated from high school. He promised his mother he would complete his schooling in the off-season and began to pack for the trip.

On a May morning in 1952, Estella Aaron made Henry a couple of sandwiches, handed him two dollar bills, hugged him as tight as she could, then watched tearfully from the front yard as Ed Scott, her husband, and her three eldest children piled into the family car and drove off toward the Mobile railroad depot. By this time, Henry was so frightened at the thought of leaving home for the first time in his life that his knees were knocking together. He entered the segregated railway station, a self-described "raggedy kid" wearing his sister Sarah's hand-me-down pants and toting a battered suitcase.

Before boarding the train that would take him to Charlotte, North Carolina—from there he would travel by bus to Winston-Salem, the Indianapolis Clowns' spring training site—Henry stopped to give everybody one last hug. It was then that Scott handed him an envelope with Bunny Downs's name scrawled across the front. Henry was told to give it to Downs as soon as he arrived in Winston-Salem. He glanced often at the envelope during the train ride to North Carolina, wondering what was written on the piece of paper inside. But he never peeked.

It was not until years later that Henry learned what Scott's brief message said: "Forget everything else about this player. Just watch his bat." ✧

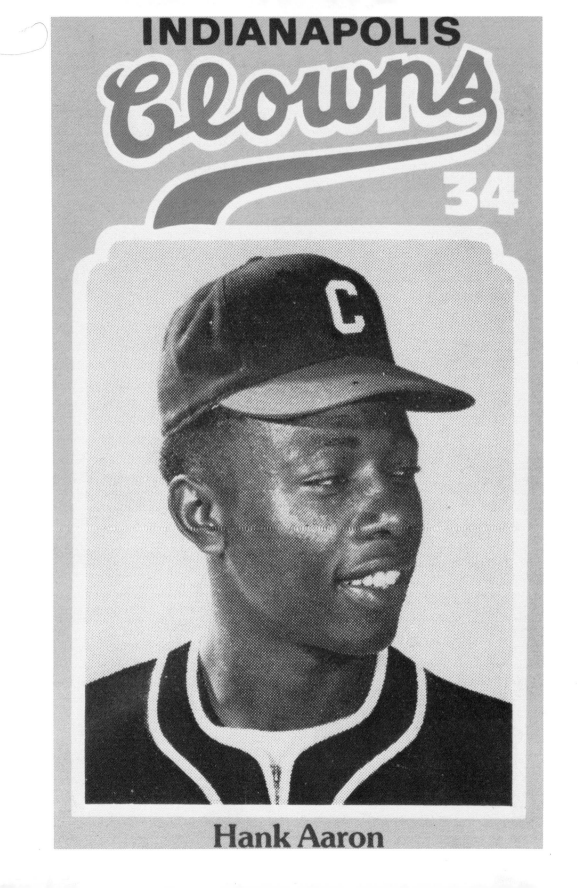

3

"IT WAS ALMOST LIKE A
FOREIGN COUNTRY"

Aaron was on his own for the first time in his life when he left Mobile in 1952 to play baseball with the Indianapolis Clowns of the Negro American League. "The older players greeted me like I was a disease," he recalled. "Most of them had been with the Clowns for several years, and they weren't greeting any green kid with open arms. A new player coming in meant that somebody had to go."

"WHERE YOU GET your equipment, kid," asked one of the veteran players, "from the Salvation Army?"

The members of the Indianapolis Clowns were not at all pleased by Henry Aaron's arrival. Seeing the 18-year-old shortstop walk into their Winston-Salem training camp meant that one of the older players would have to be cut from the squad, and the Clowns knew there were not many places where a black ballplayer could earn a living in 1952. Five years after Jackie Robinson had broken baseball's color barrier, not even half of the 16 major league teams had placed a black player on their roster. Meanwhile, the Negro leagues had begun to fail because the big leagues had become integrated, however slightly.

The Kansas City Monarchs offered the best example of black baseball's steep decline. Winners of the first modern Negro World Series, Robinson's former team had long been one of the Negro leagues' top ballclubs. Yet the fans who used to throng to Monarch games now preferred to travel across the state to St. Louis, where they could watch Robinson and the other black major leaguers compete against such white stars as Stan Musial of the hometown Cardinals.

Like the Monarchs, the Indianapolis Clowns were one of the Negro leagues' more successful teams. The Clowns originally hailed from Cincinnati and had made a name for themselves by featuring comedy routines at each ballgame. Black baseball's answer to basketball's Harlem Globetrotters, the Clowns in fact boasted Reece ("Goose") Tatum of the Globetrotters on their roster during much of the 1940s. Tatum would entertain the crowd with his lively banter and the use of such props as a three-foot-long first baseman's mitt, a bucket filled with confetti, and a woman's dress, which he would don on occasion. Richard ("King") Tut, attired in a tuxedo and top hat, and his sidekick, the dwarf Ralph ("Spec") Bebop, received top billing whenever Tatum was not around.

The ballclub officially joined the Negro American League in 1943, when the other teams realized they could boost their finances by playing regularly against the Clowns, who were an excellent drawing card. The Funmakers, as they were sometimes called by the nation's black newspapers, posted an unspectacular record during their first seven seasons in the league. When Aaron joined the club in 1952, however, the Clowns were the winners of two consecutive Eastern Division championships, and their recent string of successes only added to the players' resentment toward their young newcomer because they felt little need for a teenager's help.

Aaron tried to hold on to two thoughts as he battled his teammates' hostility and the pangs of acute homesickness. "I knew I loved to play baseball," he said. "And I had a feeling that I might be pretty good at it." In the end, these beliefs saw him through his period of adjustment.

Even if Aaron's new teammates had taken a shine to him right away, he would never have found life as a Clown to be a barrel of laughs. With a schedule that called for as many as 10 games a week in almost as many towns, the ballplayers practically lived on the team bus. "The only time we slept in a hotel was on Saturday nights," Aaron recalled. "We'd usually get to some town and stay for the weekend. After the Sunday game, it was back to that bus and the highway again."

Early in the 1952 season, the team traveled as far west as Kansas City before returning to the East Coast by way of the South. Prior to each game, Aaron remembered, "we still did the shadowball routine, taking infield practice without a baseball. But after warm-ups, the players played and left the clowning to Tut and Bebop."

Aaron, for one, proved to be all business on the diamond. Playing shortstop and batting fourth in the lineup, he got off to a fast start, hitting well over .400. With his powerful bat and steady glove keying victory after victory, his teammates quickly softened their attitude toward him. By the time the club reached the Northeast in late May, the Clowns were affectionately calling him Little Brother. To sweeten matters, he was being billed above Bebop and Tut.

Syd Pollock, the Clowns' owner, knew Aaron was a hot property and could bring in a sizable sum if his contract was sold to a major league franchise. And from what Pollock gathered, it was only a matter of time before some ballclub made a concrete offer for the infielder. The New York Giants had already put a scout on his trail, and so had a few other teams.

The Clowns' owner decided to hasten the process by contacting the Boston Braves, a club with whom he had recently had a few dealings. Pollock wrote a letter to John Mullen, the Braves' farm director, and added an enticing postscript: "We have an eighteen-year-old shortstop batting cleanup for us."

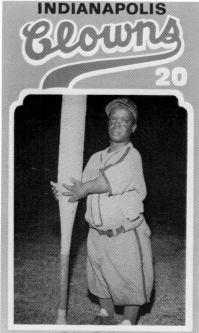

Spec BeBop

The merrymaking dwarf Ralph ("Spec") Bebop was a major reason why the Indianapolis Clowns proved to be an excellent drawing card. "We were a serious baseball team," Aaron said, "but the fans expected us to do some clowning to live up to our name. That was what made the Clowns the top attraction in the Negro leagues."

Intrigued by Pollock's comment, Mullen ordered Dewey Griggs, a scout based in Buffalo, New York, to take a look at Aaron. Griggs watched the young ballplayer's every move during a May 25 double-header that pitted the Clowns against the Memphis Red Sox in Buffalo. Aaron, the scout reported to Mullen, "looked very good. . . . This boy could be the answer."

Griggs's only real concern was Aaron's throwing arm. In the first game, the shortstop had flipped the ball to first base instead of gunning it. His underhand and sidearm tosses had prompted the scout to visit the Clowns' dugout between games so he could ask Aaron, "Can't you throw any better than that?"

"Oh, sure, I can throw any way you want it thrown," the teenager replied. "I just been throwing enough to get them out."

Griggs had one other suggestion for Aaron. "I know you're killing this kind of pitching that way, but you'll never be able to play in the big leagues batting cross-handed," the scout said. "Those pitchers will knock the bat right out of your hands. Next time you come to bat, switch your hands and try the regular grip."

Aaron experimented with the new grip during his next plate appearance and wound up smacking the ball over the fence for a home run. Upon seeing the ball leave the stadium, he decided to give up batting cross-handed for good.

Aaron's display at shortstop in the second game proved to be as impressive as his hitting. Griggs reported to Mullen after the doubleheader, "In the second game [Aaron] rifled two good overhanded throws to first and made the double play without the slightest hesitation."

Griggs took one last look at Aaron when the Clowns came to Buffalo for a Sunday doubleheader against the Monarchs. On that June afternoon,

Aaron enjoyed perhaps the most glorious day of his young career. He rapped out seven hits, including two home runs, in nine at-bats.

Griggs had seen enough, and he told Mullen to buy out Aaron's contract at once. The Braves, however, were not the only team that had decided to bid for Aaron's services. The Giants wanted him, too, and said they were willing to purchase his playing rights for $2,500—the same sum that Pollock was being offered by Mullen.

Aaron himself had the last word in the matter, for any deal would be meaningless if he refused to sign a new contract. He was not about to turn down a pay increase, however, and so he opted to join the Braves. Neither Boston nor New York had offered him a signing bonus, but the Braves had said they were willing to pay him a salary of $350 a month, which beat the Giants' deal by a cool $100.

Aaron's first taste of integrated organized baseball (middle row, far left) came in June 1952, when he teamed up with Julie Bowers (middle row, far right) and Wes Covington (back row, third from right) as the only black players with the Eau Claire Bears. "I never doubted my ability," Aaron said later, "but when you hear all your life that you're inferior, it makes you wonder if the other guys have something you've never seen before. If they do, I'm still looking for it. It didn't take long to find out that the ball was still round after it left a white pitcher's hand, and it responded the same way when you hit it with a bat."

In retrospect, New York had made one of the biggest blunders in baseball history. For only a few hundred dollars more, the Giants could have landed a perennial all-star at a bargain price. And they could have penciled Aaron's name into a lineup that boasted another Alabama native and recent star of the Negro American League: center fielder Willie Mays, who had made his major league debut with the Giants one year earlier.

As excited as Aaron was over the prospect of playing minor league ball, he was never more frightened than when it was time to leave the Clowns in mid-June 1952 and board an airplane for the first flight of his life. The rickety twin-engine craft took him, he recalled, "over a part of the country I'd hardly ever heard about, much less been to, headed for a white town to play ball with white boys." The town was Eau Claire, in central Wisconsin. The Braves had assigned him to finish the 1952 season with the Eau Claire Bears of the Northern League, a class C farm team.

The first thing Aaron did upon arriving in Eau Claire was to check into the local YMCA; by taking up residence in town, he immediately increased the local black population by 33 percent. He was somewhat comforted to find out that two of the three other blacks in Eau Claire also played ball for the Bears: Julie Bowers, a catcher, and Wes Covington, an outfielder. These two teammates eased Aaron's adjustment to life in rural Wisconsin, but only by a little bit. "We didn't exactly blend in," he remembered. "I had the feeling people were watching me, looking at me as though I were some kind of strange creature."

The isolation ate away at Aaron until he could stand it no longer. Two weeks after his arrival, he packed his bags and phoned his family to tell them he was coming home: the opportunity to play professional baseball was not worth the price of loneliness. "It was almost like being in a foreign country," he said.

"Man, are you out of your mind?" Herbert, Jr., said to his younger brother over the telephone. "I just wish I'd had the chance you got." In the end, Henry agreed to remain in Eau Claire and give integrated baseball another shot.

Aaron was soon glad that he did. Just a few days after he called home, he was picked to start at shortstop in the Northern League All-Star Game. This unexpected honor gave Aaron the boost of confidence he needed, and he wound up his first season in the minors as the league's second-leading hitter, with a .336 batting average. He also drove in 61 runs in only 87 games. These accomplishments made him the unanimous choice for the league's Rookie of the Year Award.

But Aaron's baseball season was not quite yet over. After finishing up with the Eau Claire Bears, he rejoined the Indianapolis Clowns, whose strong play in the first half of the season had enabled them to gain a berth in the 1952 Negro League World Series. The series was a best-of-13-games marathon held in a number of southern cities, including Mobile. The Clowns wound up winning the title, seven games to five, with Aaron connecting for five home runs while batting over .400. He closed out the year by returning to the Josephine Allen Institute and obtaining his high school degree, thereby keeping his promise to his mother.

With that, Aaron completed the most adventurous year of his young life. But it was nothing compared to what he would experience in 1953, when the Braves asked him to help integrate professional baseball in the Deep South. ❧

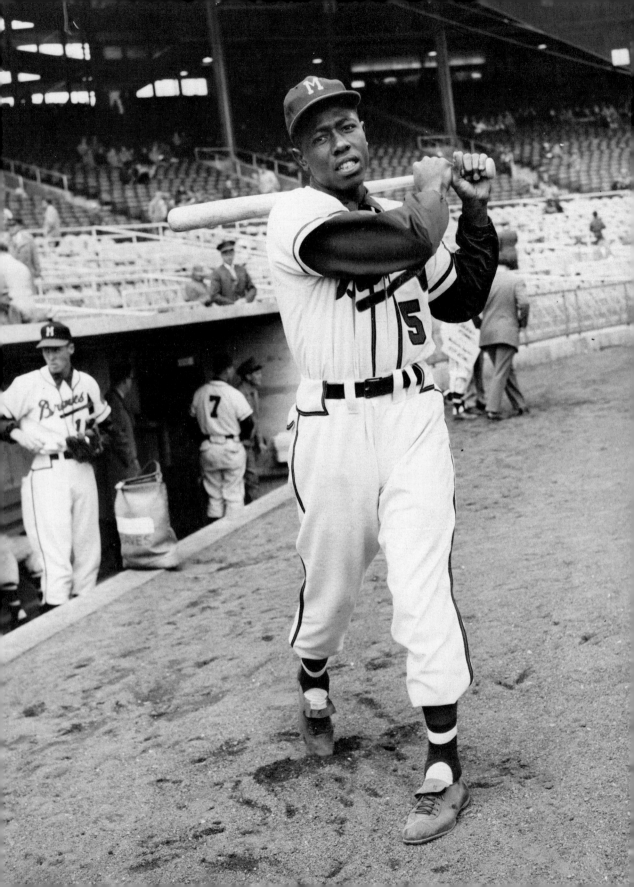

4

"HE'LL MAKE THE FANS FORGET JACKIE ROBINSON"

THE SOUTH ATLANTIC league consisted of eight teams located in Alabama, Florida, Georgia, and South Carolina. Less formally known as the Sally League, this class A minor league had been around since 1904. Nevertheless, as the spring of 1953 arrived, the circuit possessed absolutely no history in the area of improved race relations. Every one of the thousands of ballplayers who had played in the Sally League over the past half century had been white.

Up until 1946, all professional baseball leagues had remained racially segregated. But on April 18 of that year, Jackie Robinson played his first minor league game for the Brooklyn Dodgers' top farm team, the Montreal Royals of the International League, and baseball's so-called great experiment had begun in earnest. The next stage of the experiment took place the following year, on April 15, when Robinson participated in his first National League game. Eighty-one days later, Larry Doby made his debut with the Cleveland Indians and broke the American League's color barrier.

Seeing both major leagues become desegregated in 1947, most Negro league ballplayers believed they would soon be joining Robinson and Doby in the senior and junior circuits. There were "ten, twenty, thirty guys who could just step right in," recalled

Aaron loosens up before a game in 1954, his rookie major league season. "I believe that my style of hitting was developed as a result of batting against bottle caps," he said. "The way one of those things will dip and float, you've got to jump out and get it, and that's the way I always hit a baseball."

39

Monte Irvin, at one time the leading candidate to integrate professional baseball. Yet Irvin, whom most scouts rated as a better ballplayer than Robinson, failed to reach the majors until 1949. His slow rise to the New York Giants was typical of the black ballplayer's experience. Even though the face of the national pastime was changing, baseball executives believed that the mixing of the races had to proceed carefully, and it was not until 1959 that every big league team had a black player on its roster.

By the time Henry Aaron was about to begin his second season in the Braves organization, there were still two all-white circuits left in professional baseball: the Southern Association and the Sally League. The Southern Association would fold in 1961, with a black player batting only once in the league's history. The Sally League in effect became the last bastion of segregated baseball to fall in the United States.

At the tender age of 19, Aaron received word that he was slated to become one of the Sally League's integration pioneers. In the spring of 1953, the Braves organization, which was then in the process of moving its major league franchise from Boston to Milwaukee, sent him, as well as Horace Garner and Puerto Rican–born Felix Mantilla, to play for the Sally League's lone Florida team, the Jacksonville Tars. Along with Al Israel and Fleming Reedy, two black ballplayers headed for the Savannah club, they would be breaking the league's color line.

In order for black ballplayers to win a permanent place in the professional ranks, the blacks who were chosen to play alongside whites had to be extremely talented *and* highly dignified. And then they had to perform brilliantly every step of the way. In effect, every black ballplayer had to prove he was another Jackie Robinson or Larry Doby.

"We knew," Aaron recalled, "that we not only had to play well, but if we ever lost our cool or caused

"When we looked up at all those black and white faces screaming at us, we couldn't help but feel the weight of what we were doing," Aaron said of the effort to integrate the South Atlantic League during the 1953 season. Ben Geraghty (right), the Jacksonville Tars skipper, "crowded out a lot of the stuff and never let it get close," Aaron recalled. "In all the years I played baseball, I never had a manager who cared more for his players or knew more about the game."

an incident, it might set the whole program back five or ten years. When the pitchers threw at us, we had to get up and swing at the next pitch." They also had to ignore the racial slurs that some of the fans shouted at them. Having been raised in the South, Aaron was no stranger to racially motivated verbal abuse. But now he found himself being subjected daily to vicious insults and death threats.

The teenager got his revenge by playing excellent ball. "That was the only kind of recourse we had," he explained. Aaron also delighted in seeing a huge number of black faces in the stands at each game. Studying his every move, the fans in the black section would shout with glee each time he caught a fly ball or connected for a base hit.

It was impossible, however, for Aaron to counter the legalized discrimination that he faced away from the ballpark. Even though all the Tars traveled together on road trips across the Deep South, whenever the team bus stopped at a restaurant or hotel, the facility was always for whites only. Quietly, the white ballplayers would file out of the bus, leaving

What Aaron called his "ticket to the big leagues": Milwaukee Braves outfielder Bobby Thomson writhes on the ground on March 13, 1954, after sliding into second base in a spring training game and fracturing his right ankle. The injury paved the way for Aaron to make the ballclub and become the Braves' opening day left fielder.

Aaron, Garner, and Mantilla behind. Either their teammates would bring them some food, or the three of them would take their meals in the restaurant's kitchen. Barred from the whites-only hotels, the nonwhite players had to find lodgings in homes on the black side of town.

No matter where Aaron, Garner, and Mantilla stayed, Ben Geraghty, the Tars manager, would visit them. The man whom Aaron later called the best manager he ever played for wanted to make sure that all his ballplayers felt they were part of the team.

And it was quite a group of players. According to Aaron, "We had the best roster that Jacksonville had ever seen." The Tars ran away from every other club in the standings except for Columbia. Toward the end of the season, the two teams finally had a showdown, hooking up in a pair of doubleheaders. Aaron went 12 for 13 in the four games as Jacksonville swept both twin bills to clinch the Sally League pennant.

Although Jacksonville later lost to Columbia in the last round of the league playoffs, the overall campaign was, according to Aaron, a huge success. "We had shown the people of Georgia and Alabama and South Carolina and Florida that we were good ballplayers and decent human beings," he said, "and that all it took to get along together was to get a little more used to each other. We had shown them that the South wouldn't fall off the map if we played in their ballparks. At the end of the season, we still heard a few choice names being shouted at us from the stands, but not as often or as loudly as in the beginning." One *Jacksonville Journal* columnist wrote, "I seriously believe Aaron may have started Jacksonville down the road to racial understanding."

Almost as satisfying were the words of encouragement Aaron was beginning to hear from people in the Braves organization. John Mullen said that Aaron had developed into a major league hitter. Geraghty was even more lavish with his praise. "In a year or so he'll make the fans forget Jackie Robinson, and I'm not exaggerating," said the Tars manager. "He never pays attention to who's pitching. He hits them all."

Aaron did indeed. In 1953, he topped the Sally League in virtually every offensive category—batting average (.362), runs batted in (125), runs scored (115), base hits (208), total bases (338), and doubles (36)—and finished second best in both triples (14) and home runs (44). He was also voted to the Sally League's All-Star team and was named the circuit's most valuable player. "Henry Aaron," quipped one local sportswriter, "led the league in everything but hotel accommodations."

The Most Valuable Player Award was presented to Aaron at a banquet held immediately after the last playoff game. As pleased as he was to accept the honor, he had a much more pressing matter to attend to that evening. He was planning to ask the young woman he had started dating that spring if she would marry him.

Charlie Grimm, Aaron's first manager with the Milwaukee Braves, gives the 20-year-old rookie a piece of advice prior to the start of the 1954 season. "Once I got acclimated," Aaron said, "I found that playing in the big leagues wasn't nearly as hard as getting there."

The first time Aaron ever saw Barbara Lucas, she was walking to the post office down the block from the Tars' ballpark. Smitten, he asked a mutual friend to introduce them, and the next thing Henry knew, he was walking down the street with Barbara at his side. He learned that she had been a student at Florida A & M University in Tallahassee but had moved back home to attend a local business college. From then on, Aaron would walk by her family's house on his way to the stadium. "The rest of that baseball season," Aaron recalled, "I reckon I spent as much time at the Lucases' as I did at the ballpark."

When the season came to an end, so did the last stage of their courtship. Henry telephoned Barbara from the Sally League banquet and proposed to her. She consented, and they were married in Jacksonville a few days later, on October 6.

The newlyweds spent their honeymoon in Puerto Rico. The trip then turned into a working holiday, because the Braves' top brass had arranged for Aaron to play winter ball for the Caguas team in the Puerto Rican League. Convinced that the slick-fielding Mantilla was the ballclub's shortstop of the future, the Braves had shifted Aaron to second base prior to the start of the 1953 season. The switch had not been a success: the former shortstop committed 36 errors.

Now the Braves wanted to try Aaron as an outfielder. "The way we look at it," Mullen told him over the phone, "you've got too much to learn at second base, but you can make it in a much bigger hurry as an outfielder." Possessing excellent foot speed and a strong throwing arm, he seemed to have all the necessary tools that the position required.

While Aaron learned how to play the outfield in Puerto Rico, he administered a lesson in hitting to the opposing pitchers. Most of the hurlers in the Puerto Rican League boasted big league experience, but they did not intimidate Aaron in the least. He finished third in the league in batting average (.322) and tied for first in home runs (9). He even won the 60-yard dash competition held before the All-Star Game, of which he was named the most valuable player.

Boasting an impressive list of credentials compiled during his first two years in professional baseball, Aaron arrived at the Braves' 1954 spring training site in Bradenton eager to win a spot on the Milwaukee Braves' major league roster. When he took a look around the training camp, however, he realized there was no place for him to play. The Braves already possessed four experienced outfielders—Bill Bruton, Andy Pafko, Jim Pendleton, and the newly acquired Bobby Thomson—and had just traded for another second baseman, Danny O'Connell of the Pittsburgh Pirates.

Then came the break that launched the young ballplayer's big league career. On March 13, in an exhibition game against the New York Yankees in St. Petersburg, Florida, Thomson slid into second base and fractured his ankle. Aaron, who had been standing near the third-base dugout, watched some of his teammates carry Thomson off the field on a stretcher.

The following morning, the Braves' manager, Charlie Grimm, walked over to Aaron in the clubhouse. Picking up the 20-year-old's glove, he tossed it to Aaron and said, "Kid, you're my left fielder. It's yours until somebody takes it away from you."

For the next 23 years, no one did. ❧

5

"OL' HANK IS READY"

❦

Aᴦᴛᴇʀ HENRY AARON and the Milwaukee Braves ended their 1954 spring training camp in early April, the ballplayers barnstormed their way north in preparation for the opening of the baseball season. Opposing them on the exhibition tour were the Brooklyn Dodgers, who had finished the 1953 campaign 13 games in front of second-place Milwaukee. Brooklyn had captured the National League pennant the previous year as well.

A powerhouse of a team, the Dodgers featured an all-star at practically every position. In the outfield were Carl Furillo, the league's batting leader in 1953, and Edwin ("Duke") Snider, who had tied with Eddie Mathews as the league's slugging leader. First base was manned by the rock-solid Gil Hodges. Jim ("Junior") Gilliam and Harold ("Pee Wee") Reese handled the duties at second base and shortstop, respectively. And

Aiming for the pennant: The Milwaukee Braves developed into a contending ballclub in the mid-1950s with Aaron, third baseman Eddie Mathews (center), and Joe Adcock (right) supplying most of the extra-base power. Aaron hit for a high batting average as well, and by the end of the decade he had become the second-youngest player in history (after Ty Cobb) to reach 1,000 career base hits.

"I sort of trailed him like a puppy," Aaron said of Bill Bruton, the speedy Milwaukee Braves outfielder who led the National League in stolen bases from 1953 through 1955. "Bruton was sort of the 'senior officer' among the Negro players" when Aaron joined the Braves, "and he was the one who took charge of any special arrangements the black players had to make—finding restaurants, arranging cabs to the ballpark, that sort of thing."

Jackie Robinson, about to begin his eighth major league campaign, was splitting his playing time between third base and the outfield.

As good as these Dodgers were, none of them was the ballclub's most dominating player. That distinction belonged to a former Negro National League star, catcher Roy Campanella. He had hit .312 with 41 home runs and 142 runs batted in for Brooklyn in 1953. A top-notch signal caller as well, he had been named the National League's most valuable player for the second time in three years.

Two other black ballplayers—pitchers Joe Black and Don Newcombe—were on the Dodgers' roster in addition to Campanella, Gilliam, and Robinson. Together, they gave Brooklyn the most—as well as the most talented—black players of any team in the league.

The barnstorming tour certainly put Aaron in good company, and as luck would have it, one of the exhibition stops for the Dodgers and the Braves was Mobile. Aaron was delighted at the chance to suit up in his Alabama hometown. He also relished the prospect of having his father see for himself what had resulted from the promise Henry had made six years earlier; he had indeed become a major leaguer before Jackie Robinson had retired. Wearing a Milwaukee uniform with the number 5 on his jersey, the 20-year-old rookie celebrated the afternoon by rapping out a pair of base hits at Hartwell Field.

Aaron may have felt sky-high about being a major leaguer, but he tried to keep a low profile off the ballfield. "I didn't go around making myself the life of the clubhouse," he recalled. "I came to the Braves on business, and I intended to see that business was good."

To ease his transition into the big leagues, Aaron made it a point to spend time with the black Dodgers in the segregated hotels where both teams lodged as they traveled north. For the most part, he listened to their conversations and kept silent, learning from the veterans what to expect from life in the National League. "Those hotel rooms," he acknowledged later, "were my college."

Bill Bruton, about to begin his second season with the Braves, took over as Aaron's adviser when the ballclub reached Milwaukee. The chief lesson the black center fielder hammered home to Aaron was that baseball's great experiment was not over. The major leagues did not have room for black players who performed at a mediocre level. "I'd better be good," Aaron realized, "or I'd be gone."

He was not good right away. Extremely anxious to do well in his first big league game, Aaron was guilty of overswinging and wound up hitless in five times at bat against the Cincinnati Reds. It was not until two days later, on April 15, at Milwaukee County Stadium, that he recorded his first major league hit, a double off pitcher Vic Raschi of the St. Louis Cardinals.

Aaron faced Raschi again eight days later, on a Friday night in St. Louis. As the rookie left fielder dug his spikes into the batter's box for his second plate appearance of the game, none of the spectators at Sportsman's Park had any inkling that they were about to witness a historic moment. But when Aaron connected in the fourth inning for his first major league home run, a solo shot that cleared the left-field fence, the greatest chase in baseball history had commenced.

Aaron hit only 12 more home runs in his first big league season—certainly not enough to indicate the mighty numbers that would soon follow. His entire rookie campaign, in fact, ended on a disappointing note. On September 5, with one month left to play in the 1954 season and Milwaukee just five games out of first place, Aaron slid into third base for a triple

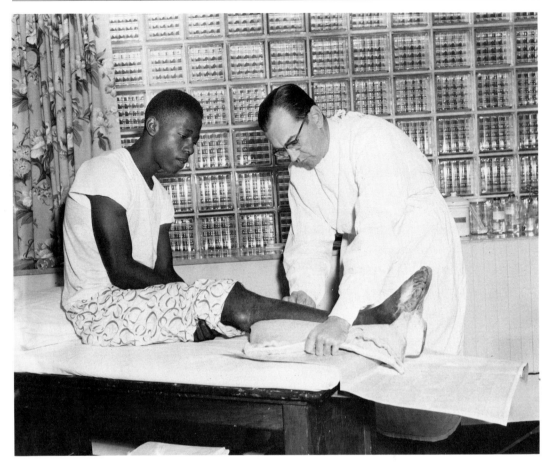

A Milwaukee physician removes Aaron's leg cast on November 9, 1954, two months after he broke his right ankle while sliding into third base during his rookie campaign. "By the end of the season," Aaron recalled, "I knew I belonged in the big leagues, but I was a little disappointed in myself. It was probably because I figured I ought to lead any league I played in."

and broke his ankle when his spikes got caught in the bag. The fracture helped silence the Braves' pennant hopes and ended Aaron's season with a .280 batting average, 27 doubles, and 69 runs batted in.

Those numbers would have satisfied most rookies. "Not if you've been used to hitting .340 all your life," Aaron told a Milwaukee sportswriter. Eager to raise the level of his game, the injured ballplayer waited impatiently for his leg cast to come off that November. As soon as it did, he returned to Mobile, grabbed a bat and a few balls, and dragged his brother Tommie into Carver Park for a batting-practice session. Back in Henry's old stamping ground, 15-year-old Tommie fed his elder brother a steady diet of change-ups—

the pitch he had had trouble with all season. They repeated this session daily until spring training arrived and Henry announced he was ready for opening day.

So were the Milwaukee fans, who had set another National League attendance record in the Braves' second season in Wisconsin. In 1955, the Milwaukee rooters would again swarm past the brick-face portals of Milwaukee County Stadium, confident that their team would improve on its disappointing third-place finish in 1954. And why not? The ballclub was loaded with talent.

In addition to Aaron, the Braves boasted two of the game's top players: perennial 20-game-winner Warren Spahn and power-hitting third baseman Eddie Mathews. Another mighty slugger, first baseman Joe Adcock, and the sure-handed double-play combination of second baseman Danny O'Connell and shortstop Johnny Logan rounded out a strong infield. Del Crandall, one of the best-hitting catchers in the league, handled the chores behind home plate.

A talented bunch of outfielders backed up the infielders. Bill Bruton, Milwaukee's speedy center fielder, had led the league in stolen bases in each of the last two years. The hard-hitting Bobby Thomson, fully recovered from his leg injury, had returned to left field, sending Andy Pafko to the bench. Over in right field, where his superb defensive play would soon earn him a trio of Gold Glove Awards, was Henry Aaron. (To help commemorate his newest spot in the outfield, his fourth position in four years, Aaron switched his uniform number to 44.)

The Braves' starting lineup was complemented by arguably the best pitching staff in the league. The anchor was Spahn, who would ultimately post the most career victories by a left-hander in baseball history. Hurlers Bob Buhl, Lew Burdette, and Gene Conley filled out Milwaukee's imposing rotation, while bullpen ace Ernie Johnson headed up the relief corps. All told, it was a young and talented crew, and Manager Charlie Grimm expected his players to challenge the Dodgers and Willie Mays's New York Giants for the pennant.

As great as the expectations were, the Braves' 1955 campaign turned sour quickly. Brooklyn bolted out to a huge early lead and never eased up. Milwaukee finished the season a distant second, 13½ games off the pace.

Aaron, however, was hardly to blame for the Braves' disappointing season. He batted .314 (sixth best in the National League), posted a circuit-leading 37 doubles, hit 27 homers, scored 105 runs, and knocked in 106 runners. He even started 27 games at second base, filling in for O'Connell when he was hurt.

The ballclub named Aaron its most valuable player at the end of the 1955 season. By then, he had already caught the attention of his fellow National Leaguers. Opposing pitchers had begun to throw at him, as they did with all imposing hitters. (They soon learned that Aaron was a more dangerous hitter after he had been knocked down.) His peers also voiced their respect for him by voting him onto the National League's 1955 All-Star squad. This honor would be bestowed on Aaron every year for the next two decades, until he joined Willie Mays in setting the all-time record for most All-Star Game appearances (24).

Because Aaron and Mays had much in common—they could run, throw, and hit as well as anyone in the league; and they had been born in the South, were nearly the same age, and were black—they were thought to be in competition with one another. In actuality, they were not rivals at all. Aaron joined a black barnstorming ballclub that Mays had assembled right after the 1955 season

ended, and the two outfielders, traveling together across the country, quickly formed a lasting friendship.

Besides Aaron and Mays, the squad included such standout big leaguers as Ernie Banks, Roy Campanella, Larry Doby, Monte Irvin, and Don Newcombe. "We didn't lose," Aaron recalled. "Ever." The team, however, had not been put together simply so it could crush its opponents. The tradition of organizing a touring all-star team of black major leaguers had been started by Jackie Robinson and carried on by Campanella. Barnstorming provided a tremendous boost to these players' incomes: they would tour for a month and take in several thousand dollars apiece, which was about a third of what they earned during the regular season.

The Braves, for example, offered to raise Aaron's annual salary after the 1955 season to $13,500—a far

"That might have been the best team ever assembled," Aaron said of the black barnstorming club that Willie Mays organized after the 1955 World Series ended. "I know I never saw a better one." The squad included (bottom row, left to right) Jim Gilliam, Hank Thompson, Mays, Sam Jones, Gene Baker, Ernie Banks, Monte Irvin; (top row, left to right) Don Newcombe, Joe Black, George Crowe, Aaron, Brooks Lawrence, Charlie White, Connie Johnson, Larry Doby, and Louis Louden.

A familiar sight to Milwaukee Braves fans in 1955: Aaron slides safely across home plate. That year, he recalled, "was the first time I hit more than twenty home runs, which was something I did for twenty straight seasons. It was also the first time I hit .300, which I would do ten times over the course of eleven seasons. It was the first time I scored 100 runs, which I did for thirteen years in a row, and drove in 100, which I did eleven times. And it was the first time I wore number 44 on my back."

cry from the multimillion-dollar figure a player of his caliber would earn a generation later. His modest income prompted him not only to join Mays's all-star team but to take another job after the barnstorming tour. Upon returning to Mobile, he became physical fitness director for the city's recreation department, working closely with the youngsters at Carver Park.

An added benefit of these postseason activities was that they kept Aaron in top shape. That the 22-year-old was in midseason form became instantly clear when he stepped into the batting cage for the first time in the spring of 1956 and lined balls all over the field. "Ol' Hank is ready," he pronounced to the observers around the cage.

Aaron had always packed a wallop into his 5-foot-11-inch, 180-pound frame. But 1956 proved to be his best year yet. He hit for a .328 average and became the second-youngest batting champion in National League history. He also paced the league in base hits (200) and doubles (34) and reached the 20-homer plateau for the second season in a row. Incredibly, it would be another 19 years before he failed to clout at least that many home runs.

Aaron later attributed his success as a hitter to his ability to concentrate on the pitcher. He would stay up nights, he said, "thinking about the pitcher I was going to face the next day. I used to play every pitcher in my mind before I went to the ballpark. I started getting ready for every game the minute I woke up."

After Aaron had carefully evaluated a hurler's strengths and weaknesses, he would wait for a certain pitch and then attack it. "Suppose a pitcher has three good pitches—a fastball, a curve, and a slider," he said. "What I do, after a lot of consideration and analyzing and studying, is to eliminate two of those pitches. . . . The chances are that I'll eventually get what I'm looking for." Aaron "often hit good pitchers the best," he added, because they were able to put the ball exactly where he expected it to be.

On those occasions when Aaron swung at a ball that was not "the pitcher's pitch," he relied heavily on his physical skills. "One thing I had in my favor was that I had strong hands and wrists, which enabled me to adjust quickly if I guessed wrong," he said. "Another advantage I had—and all good hitters have—was my eyesight. Sometimes, I could read the pitcher's grip on the ball before he ever released it and be able to tell what pitch he was throwing."

Aaron did not *always* get the pitch he was expecting or make the proper adjustments; in 1956, he uncharacteristically got off to a bad start. The Braves, however, did just the opposite. "We were in first place the whole month of May," he recalled. "Then, whatever we had going for us we lost." The ballclub tumbled all the way into the bottom half of the standings.

On June 16, John Quinn, Milwaukee's general manager, made a move to revive the staggering club. He fired Charlie Grimm and brought in Fred Haney, one of the coaches, to handle the field-general duties. The change in managers seemed to spark the ballplayers; they immediately embarked on an 11-game winning streak and reclaimed first place. After that, Aaron said, "the whole state became excited about the Braves. There were Braves hairdos and Braves cocktails and Braves banners stretched across the streets. Everybody thought we'd make it to the World Series, including the players."

Heading into the final weekend of the season, Milwaukee held a one-game lead over Brooklyn. "We had it," Aaron remembered. "It was right there in our laps." And then, like a relief pitcher giving up a game-winning home run in the bottom of the ninth inning, they let the pennant slip away. The Braves lost on Friday night to the St. Louis Cardinals, 5–4, and on Saturday dropped another one-run contest, 2–1, this time in 12 innings. The clubhouse afterward, Aaron recalled, "was the quietest one I'd ever heard."

Milwaukee managed to take the last game of the series, 4–2, but by then the damage was done. Brooklyn, playing at home in Ebbets Field, closed out a weekend sweep by winning its final ballgame against the Pittsburgh Pirates. The 1956 season ended with the Dodgers perched again on top of the National League, this time just a mere game ahead of the Braves.

As Aaron and his teammates cleaned out their lockers and said their good-byes for the winter, Haney strode into the clubhouse. "Get good and rested," he said coolly to the players, "because when you get to Bradenton next year, you're going to have one helluva spring."

6

"THE KING OF WISCONSIN"

❧

Iᴛ WAS A good thing for Henry Aaron that he arrived in excellent condition at the Milwaukee Braves' 1957 spring training site. Fred Haney, the team's manager, worked his ballplayers especially hard that spring. Even though Aaron was the National League's reigning batting champion and one of baseball's rising stars, Haney refused to treat the 23-year-old outfielder any differently than Lew Burdette, Eddie Mathews, Warren Spahn, or the other Milwaukee players.

"We ran sprints and did push-ups and sit-ups," Aaron recalled. "It was sort of a new concept for baseball, and to us it made Haney seem more like a drill sergeant than a field manager." Whenever Aaron or one of his teammates made an error during practice, "everyone dropped what he was doing and took a lap around the park."

Haney wanted his players to perform flawlessly because the previous year they had been less than perfect—and it had cost them dearly. In 1956, the Braves had possessed what their manager felt was the best team in the National League, only to see them

Aaron spearheads the Milwaukee Braves' pennant drive in the final month of the 1957 season and displays the form that soon earned him the National League's Most Valuable Player Award. He later described 1957 as "the best year of my baseball life, and it went along with the best year of baseball that any city ever had."

fall out of first place and lose the pennant to the Brooklyn Dodgers on the last weekend of the season. Haney wanted to make certain that the 1957 pennant race had a much more favorable outcome.

Aaron enjoyed a superb spring training exhibition schedule, pounding out one base hit after another, and he continued to hammer opposing pitchers as the 1957 season began on April 16 at Chicago's Wrigley Field. Batting second in the lineup, he posted an average near the .400 mark and helped the Braves win 9 of their first 10 games. In May, Haney decided to move Aaron into the cleanup spot—sandwiching him between two other sluggers, Eddie Mathews and Joe Adcock—to take advantage of the tremendous home run power the star right fielder was beginning to display at the plate.

"I honestly didn't consider myself a home run hitter," Aaron said of his early years as a ballplayer. He possessed a lightning-quick swing and the ability to hit with authority to all fields. But he had not yet connected with great frequency for home runs.

That all changed in 1957. "I think the extra home runs," Aaron said later, "were just the result of a guy getting a little older, a little stronger, figuring out the pitchers a little better." By the end of May, just a quarter of the way into the campaign, he had already socked 12 home runs.

As the season wore on, however, the grueling schedule began to take its toll on Aaron and the Braves. In 1957, one year before the Brooklyn Dodgers and New York Giants moved to the West Coast, the schedule called for Milwaukee to play 154 games over the course of 167 days. Even with a red-hot Aaron anchoring a power-packed lineup, the Braves were unable to maintain the pace of their early success. After their fast start, they established a pattern of losing several games, then winning the

Fred Haney (center), in his first full season as the Milwaukee Braves manager, seems pleased to have Aaron and second baseman Red Schoendienst (left) on his side—and for good reason. In Aaron and Schoendienst, the 1957 Braves boasted two of the top vote-getters for the National League's Most Valuable Player Award.

next few—just enough to hold on to their first-place lead.

On June 14, the day before the major league trading deadline, the team's record stood at 32–21. The Cincinnati Reds were only one and a half games back, with the Philadelphia Phillies and the Brooklyn Dodgers following closely behind. Eager to widen the slim gap, the Milwaukee crew arrived in Philadelphia that Friday to open a weekend series against the Phillies at Connie Mack Stadium. Aaron bombed his 17th homer of the season to pace a Braves victory, then returned with his teammates to the Warwick Hotel, where he learned that his club had just concluded a major deal. Milwaukee pitcher Ray Crone, second baseman Danny O'Connell, and left fielder Bobby Thomson had been traded to the New York Giants for an aging star: 34-year-old Red Schoendienst.

The Braves had been looking for a quality second baseman for a number of years; in Schoendienst, a future Hall of Famer, they obtained one of the best. Haney promptly penciled the second sacker's name into the number two spot in the lineup. "He made our team complete," Aaron said of the switch-hitting

Pitching ace Warren Spahn (left) and rookie sensation Bob Hazle (right) display a baseball for each of the home runs they hit on August 26, 1957, to help the Milwaukee Braves maintain their hold on first place. The playful mood in the clubhouse began to fade a week later, when the Braves went into a tailspin that nearly cost them the pennant.

redhead, "and after the trade it looked as though nothing would stop us."

Nevertheless, the Braves express began to derail exactly one week after the trade. In a game against the Giants, Adcock broke his ankle while sliding into second base and was sidelined until mid-September. Aaron did his best to pick up the team in Adcock's absence, and he was leading both leagues in batting average (.347), runs batted in (73), runs scored (64), and home runs (27) when the regular season halted for the All-Star break. Yet the lofty numbers Aaron compiled through July 7 were not enough to keep Milwaukee on top. The club went 12–13 after the Schoendienst trade and trailed the St. Louis Cardinals by two and a half games at midseason.

The Braves' fortunes continued to decline when the team returned to action on July 11. Aaron watched with horror from right field as his two best friends on the squad, Bill Bruton and Felix Mantilla, collided at full speed while chasing a looping fly ball into shallow left-center field. The impact—"like two sports-model cars running together," Aaron recalled—left Bruton with torn ligaments in his right knee; he never played another inning in 1957. Mantilla fared somewhat better; although the collision hospitalized him with a bruised chest, he missed only a few games.

To compensate for Bruton being out of the lineup, Haney realigned the Milwaukee outfield. Aaron was shifted to center field; Andy Pafko, who had taken over in left field for the departed Bobby Thomson, was moved to right; and rookie Wes Covington was assigned to left. With Covington supplying extra clout to the offense, the Braves put together a five-game winning streak and on July 21 moved back into first place.

Bob Hazle made sure the ballclub stayed there. On July 28, the Braves called him up from their

Wichita farm team to platoon with an ailing Pafko, and 12 days later, after a pitch hit Pafko on the elbow and forced him out of the lineup, Hazle became the everyday right fielder. At about the same time, a hurricane appeared on the Atlantic seaboard that the U.S. Weather Bureau named Hazel; for the Braves, the name instantly proved prophetic. Hurricane Hazle, as Milwaukee's 27-year-old rookie was soon being called, "hit town with a bigger bang than any bench warmer you ever heard of," remembered Aaron. Playing in 41 games, Hazle batted at an astonishing .403 clip and helped carry the Braves through the remainder of the season.

Aaron continued to shoulder his share of the burden, even though he was slowed by a sprained ankle and still coping with the switch to center field. On August 16, he belted his 33rd and 34th home runs of the season to power Milwaukee to its 10th straight triumph, an 8–1 win over Cincinnati. The victory extended the Braves' lead over the slumping Cardinals to 8½ games, with 40 left to play. "It looked like we were destined to blow everybody away," Aaron recalled.

The Milwaukee rooters were not nearly so confident. They knew the Braves had failed miserably down the stretch the previous year—and as if on cue, the team was dealt a severe blow the very next afternoon. On August 17, the same day that St. Louis slugger Stan Musial passed Aaron in the batting race, an injury forced Milwaukee shortstop Johnny Logan out of the lineup. With the Braves now missing yet another veteran player, the other clubs were able to climb back into the pennant hunt.

Milwaukee maintained a seven-game lead until the end of August, then began to stagger after Labor Day, dropping 8 of their next 11 games. Two of those defeats came on September 15, when the Braves lost both ends of a Sunday doubleheader to the Cardinals.

Aaron's "shiningest hour" began precisely at 11:34 P.M. on September 23, 1957, when he belted a curveball over Milwaukee County Stadium's center-field fence for a pennant-winning home run. "I galloped around the bases, and when I touched home plate, the whole team was there to pick me up and carry me off the field," he said. "I've never had another feeling like that."

The sweep enabled St. Louis to creep within two and a half games of first place.

Aaron was determined not to let the year become a repeat of 1956, and he spearheaded a much-needed seven-game Milwaukee winning streak. The Braves' next opponents were the Cardinals, who came to town to begin the last week of the regular season. By then, Milwaukee was in a position where a victory over St. Louis would clinch the National League pennant. "It was the first game of the big series with the Cardinals, their last chance," Aaron remembered of that Monday night meeting. "All we had to do was win one from St. Louis and that would lock it up."

When the Braves had flown back to Milwaukee the previous September after losing all hope for a league title, 20,000 loyal fans had turned out at the airport to greet them. The hometown show of support had, if anything, increased in 1957. A sellout crowd of 40,936 packed Milwaukee County Stadium on September 23, despite a night that was so cold and blustery the St. Louis relievers started a bonfire in the visiting bullpen to keep themselves warm.

The fire continued to blaze as the game headed into extra innings. But at precisely 11:34 P.M., Aaron extinguished the Cardinals' flame for the season. With the score knotted, 2–2, in the bottom of the 11th inning, he connected with a Billy Muffett curveball and drove the pitch more than 400 feet; it landed beyond the center-field fence for Aaron's 43rd round-tripper of the year. The game-ending, pennant-winning home run inspired his teammates to mob him. Overjoyed, they lifted Aaron up and carried him off the field "like I'd been named the King of Wisconsin." It was, he said later, "my shiningest hour."

Featured on the front page of the next day's Milwaukee newspapers, alongside a photograph of Aaron's teammates carrying him off the field in triumph, was a picture of a different kind of mob scene: a riot in Little Rock, Arkansas. Angry whites had resorted to violence to prevent nine black students from entering all-white Central High and desegregating the school. The Little Rock photograph did not escape Aaron's notice. Just four years after he had followed in Jackie Robinson's footsteps by helping to integrate professional baseball in the Deep South, the clock seemed to be running backward. ❧

7

"IT DOESN'T GET
ANY BETTER THAN
MILWAUKEE"

O N SEPTEMBER 24, 1957, the day after the Milwaukee Braves clinched their first National League pennant, Henry Aaron hit his 44th and final home run of the season—a grand slam—off Sam Jones of the St. Louis Cardinals. The blast not only enabled Aaron to capture his first home run title but assured him of leading the league in runs batted in (132), runs scored (118), and total bases (369). The only major offensive category in which he did not pace the league was batting average, where his .322 mark placed him third, behind two of the ballplayers he admired most, Stan Musial and Willie Mays. Aaron's failure to win the batting title cost him the prestigious Triple Crown.

"I was disappointed that I wasn't a Triple Crown man," he admitted, "but the World Series was not without one." Mickey Mantle, the switch-hitting center fielder of the American League champion New York Yankees, had accomplished the feat one year earlier. And although Mantle had failed to win a second Triple Crown in 1957, he had performed spectacularly during the season, posting a career-best .365 batting average.

Playing in his first World Series game, on October 2, 1957, Aaron chases after Hank Bauer's run-scoring single in the fifth inning at Yankee Stadium. Heavily favored to defend their World Series title against the Milwaukee Braves, who were making their first appearance in the Fall Classic, the New York Yankees won the opening contest, 3–1.

Led by (from left to right) catcher Yogi Berra, pitcher Whitey Ford, and outfielder Mickey Mantle, the star-studded New York Yankees faced the Milwaukee Braves in both the 1957 and the 1958 World Series. The Yankees were clearly baseball's most dominant team during the 1950s, winning eight pennants and six world championships.

Mantle was clearly the Yankees' most dangerous hitter, yet he was not the only team member who dominated league play. Managed by the game's shrewdest skipper, the irrepressible Casey Stengel, the New Yorkers boasted a star-studded collection of talent that featured catcher Yogi Berra (already a three-time winner of the Most Valuable Player Award) and southpaw hurler Whitey Ford (in the process of recording the 20th century's all-time highest winning percentage). Indeed, the combined efforts of the 1957 Bronx Bombers had made them the American League's best hitting *and* pitching team.

Even more impressive, the club had just captured its eighth pennant in the last nine years. And if the Yankees won the 1957 World Series, they would lay claim to their 18th world championship—three times as many as any other team. With the Milwaukee Braves appearing in their very first Fall Classic, the Yankees, the reigning world champions, were regarded as heavy favorites to defend their title.

True to form, New York took two of the first three games and delivered what appeared to be the knock-out punch in Game 4 of the best-of-seven series. And they did it in typically stunning fashion. In the bottom of the fourth inning on a windy Sunday afternoon at Milwaukee County Stadium, Aaron smacked a three-run homer to give his club a 3–1 advantage. Warren Spahn then showed the bulldog determination that had made him the National League's winningest pitcher in 1957. Spahn had far from his best stuff, yet he kept the New Yorkers off balance and at bay, and they trailed, 4–1, going into the top of the ninth inning.

"I could see people filing out of the ball park as the Yankees came to bat," Aaron recalled. "They were heading for their cars, pretty sure that the Braves had won and tied the series at two games apiece." The mad scramble for the exits continued as Spahn retired two of the first four batters. Then came the crushing blow. With Milwaukee just one out away from victory, New York catcher Elston Howard stepped up to the plate and drilled a three-run homer over the left-field fence.

"We could have folded then," Aaron said of the game-tying homer. "You never saw a quieter dugout in your life when we came in from the field. We all looked as if we'd been watching a murder."

An eerie silence engulfed the stadium as the Braves failed to score in the bottom half of the inning. A handful of pitches later, in the top of the 10th, the shocked hometown fans sat in absolute despair as they watched Yankees outfielder Hank Bauer triple home infielder Tony Kubek. "It began to look as if we were dead for the whole series," Aaron recalled, "as well as the fourth game."

Attempting to stir something up, Manager Fred Haney called on Nippy Jones, a journeyman ballplayer, to bat for Spahn. Haney was instantly rewarded for his choice. Right-hander Tommy Byrne uncorked the first pitch low and inside to Jones; it

The turning point of the 1957 World Series: With the Milwaukee Braves trailing, 5–4, in the bottom of the 10th inning of Game 4, home-plate umpire Augie Donatelli awards pinch hitter Nippy Jones (far right) first base after detecting a smudge of shoe polish on the baseball. The Braves proceeded to rally for three runs in the inning and evened the World Series at two games apiece.

skidded in the dirt and skipped past Howard crouching behind home plate. The pitch was called a ball, prompting Jones to spin around and argue that the pitch had hit him. As proof, he picked up the baseball, which had caromed off the backstop and rolled conveniently to his feet, and handed it to home-plate umpire Augie Donatelli. A scuff mark of black shoe polish convinced Donatelli that the pitch had brushed Jones's spikes, and the umpire awarded him first base.

"I don't think anybody in America would have imagined that the guy who would turn the Series around would be Nippy Jones," Aaron said. Just the same, seeing Jones reach base inspired the Braves. Red Schoendienst, batting against reliever Bob Grim, sacrificed pinch runner Felix Mantilla to second. The next hitter, Johnny Logan, ripped a double into the left-field corner and drove Mantilla home to even the score at 5–5.

With the remaining fans cheering wildly, Eddie Mathews, held hitless in the first three games, approached the batter's box; at the same time, Aaron moved into the on-deck circle. His team's hottest hitter, Aaron would be the only player on either squad to get a base hit in every game of the series. As Mathews adjusted his stance at home plate, he knew

Lew Burdette puts the Milwaukee Braves within one victory of their first world championship by blanking the New York Yankees, 1–0, in Game 5 on October 7, 1957. He returned to the mound just three days later and clinched the World Series by tossing his second consecutive shutout. "Burdette," Aaron noted, "had been traded by the Yankees before he ever got a chance to really pitch for them, and he hadn't forgotten it."

that the Yankees wanted to pitch around Aaron, which meant that Grim would have to challenge *him*.

Seeking to end the game with one swing, the Milwaukee third baseman zeroed in on Grim's first offering and drove the pitch deep to left. From his spot in the on-deck circle, Aaron watched the ball soar into the late-afternoon sky and held his breath as he followed its downward flight. The ball landed foul.

Swinging at the next pitch, Mathews lifted another long drive, this time along the right-field line. His second mighty shot again teased the crowd. The ball streaked toward the bleachers before veering into foul territory, barely missing a home run.

Now that he had a two-strike advantage on the Braves' third baseman, Grim tried to entice him to swing at a ball outside the strike zone. Mathews looked over each of the next two pitches carefully and let them both sail wide.

On his next delivery, Grim attempted to slip a fastball over the plate but put the pitch in the wrong spot. Mathews uncoiled his body into a perfectly timed swing and arced a two-run homer into the right-field bleachers. The blow gave Milwaukee a come-from-behind, 7–5 victory. "After that," Aaron said, "we felt like we couldn't be beaten."

World Series heroes Lew Burdette (left) and Warren Spahn (right) throw confetti into the air during what Aaron called "the damnedest parade you ever saw. I suppose that if you've seen one World Series celebration you've seen them all," he said, "but I kind of doubt that, when I stop to think again of Milwaukee on the night of October 10, 1957."

The only problem was that the Yankees felt the same way. At Milwaukee County Stadium the following afternoon, the two clubs battled like warring armies refusing to give up ground. During the first five innings of Game 5, neither team permitted the opposition to cross the plate. Then, in the bottom of the sixth inning, Aaron poked a base hit that sent Mathews scampering into third and set up the game's only tally: a run-scoring single by Joe Adcock.

The biggest hero of the Braves' victory, however, was their starter, Lew Burdette. The 30-year-old hurler went the full nine innings in outdueling Whitey Ford, 1–0, to push the National League champs ahead in the series, three games to two.

"All we needed was one game," Aaron recalled, and he put Milwaukee a step closer to clinching their first World Series when both teams returned to Yankee Stadium two days later for Game 6. With the Braves trailing 2–1 in the top of the seventh inning,

Aaron tied the ballgame with his third homer of the series. Just as timely, Hank Bauer hit a solo shot in the bottom of the inning to unknot the score. And when the Yankees' starting pitcher, Bob Turley, held the visitors in check over the final two innings, the stage was set for what promised to be a memorable affair: a climactic seventh game.

Much to everyone's surprise, the final contest of the 1957 World Series contained relatively little drama. Milwaukee jumped out to a big lead by scoring four runs in the third inning; and Lew Burdette, pitching on only two days' rest (in place of a flu-weakened Warren Spahn), performed like Hall of Famers Walter Johnson and Cy Young rolled into one. Putting on another masterful display, Burdette held New York scoreless on a meager seven hits.

The Bronx Bombers were stunned by the 5–0 whitewash. They had been shut out only once during the regular season. And now, within a span of just four days, Burdette had blanked them twice.

Having hurled two consecutive shutouts and three complete-game victories, Burdette was voted the 1957 World Series' most valuable player. But the award could just as easily have gone to Aaron. The home run champion's .393 batting average, 11 hits, 3 homers, 7 runs batted in, and 22 total bases were the highest totals on either squad.

Aaron received his due a few weeks later, when the National League named him its most valuable player. The honor awed the 23-year-old star, as did the thought of seeing his name listed next to those of Roy Campanella, Willie Mays, Don Newcombe, and Jackie Robinson in baseball's record book. To win the World Series and then finish the season among such impressive company led Aaron to proclaim, "It doesn't get any better than Milwaukee in 1957."

8

"WE WERE THE
SUPERIOR TEAM"

⚜

THE MILWAUKEE BRAVES never did match
the success of their 1957 season, although they came
close each of the next two years.

In 1958, Henry Aaron, Lew Burdette, Eddie
Mathews, and Warren Spahn led the way as Milwaukee repeated as National League champions, winning the pennant by eight games over the Pittsburgh
Pirates. Aaron, trying to measure up to his previous
season's performance, hit .326 (fourth best in the
league) with 30 home runs (fifth best) and 95 runs
batted in (sixth best). His final totals were impressive
enough for him to finish as the third-leading vote-
getter for the Most Valuable Player Award behind
Ernie Banks of the Chicago Cubs and Willie Mays.

Aaron then picked up in postseason play right
where he had left off, compiling the second-highest
batting average (.333) in the 1958 World Series. This

*The National League's most valuable player in 1957 surveys the
action at Chicago's Wrigley Field alongside Cubs shortstop Ernie
Banks, who won the MVP Award in 1958 and 1959. "We looked
out for each other, passed along information," Banks said of his
relationship with Aaron. "We did the same thing with Mays and the
others. Some of it went back to the friendships we made barnstorming, but where we really were able to stay up with each other was
meeting every year at the All-Star Game."*

Warren Spahn is congratulated by the Milwaukee Braves top brass after shutting out the New York Yankees on two hits in Game 4 of the 1958 World Series. The 3–0 triumph put the Braves within a victory of their second consecutive world title and prompted Aaron to say of Spahn, "It looked as though he would do what [Lew] Burdette had done the year before."

time around, the Fall Classic, which again pitted the Braves against the New York Yankees, did not suggest a meeting between David and Goliath. "The two of us were far and away the class of our leagues," Aaron recalled, "and we knew that if we could beat them twice in a row we would clearly establish ourselves as the best team in baseball."

Spahn and Burdette, both of them 20-game winners during the regular season, pointed Milwaukee in the right direction. Spahn posted a complete-game victory in the opening contest, and Burdette did the same in Game 2. After Don Larsen and Ryne Duren combined to shut out the Braves on October 4, Spahn blanked the New Yorkers on just two base hits the following afternoon and put Milwaukee ahead in the series, three games to one. Not since 1925 had a team in the Yankees' position bounced back to win a World Series, so the Braves refused to panic when

Bob Turley shut *them* out in Game 5. All Milwaukee had to do was split the two remaining games at Milwaukee County Stadium and the World Series would be theirs.

Much to the hometown fans' dismay, there was no final hurrah. In Game 6, the Yankees battled the Braves evenly through nine innings, 2–2, then eked out a 4–3 victory in the next frame. The following afternoon, October 9, another tight ballgame unfolded. With the score again deadlocked at 2–2 and the world championship hanging on every pitch, Elston Howard singled in one run and Bill ("Moose") Skowron homered for three more in the top of the eighth inning. Turley then recorded the final six Milwaukee outs without allowing a run, and the Braves' dreams of glory faded with the setting sun.

It was a bitter defeat for the Milwaukee players and their fans. The team had lost the last three games of the World Series when the title was within easy reach. "What happened in that series," Aaron said later, "was sort of a tip-off on what was about to happen to the Braves over a period of seasons."

In spite of the sudden letdown the previous autumn, Milwaukee entered the 1959 campaign as a heavy favorite to win its third straight pennant, a feat that only four other National League teams had accomplished since the World Series was first held in 1903. The Braves got off to a fast start, and by the second month of the season they had built up a four-and-a-half-game lead.

Meanwhile, the team's 25-year-old right fielder was hitting everything in sight. "I always felt that some year Hank Aaron would hit .400," said Spahn. It appeared that 1959 would be the year. "I was seeing the ball so well," Aaron recalled, "that I stopped going to movies for a while, because I didn't want anything to affect my eyes." He batted .508 during April and was still above the .450 mark nearly

Pittsburgh Pirates manager Danny Murtaugh (left) attempts to console a disappointed Harvey Haddix (right) as the pitcher leaves the Milwaukee County Stadium field after suffering perhaps the most heartbreaking defeat in baseball history. Haddix had tossed a record 12 perfect innings against the Milwaukee Braves on the night of May 26, 1959, only to lose the game, 1–0, in the bottom of the 13th inning.

a month later, when the Braves opened a series against the Pirates on May 26 at Milwaukee County Stadium.

Despite an overcast sky streaked with flashes of lightning, nearly 20,000 fans arrived at the ballpark on that Tuesday night to watch the league's defending champions battle the runners-up. Burdette was on the mound for Milwaukee; Harvey ("the Kitten") Haddix was the Pittsburgh hurler. Together, these two pitchers were about to fashion one of the most remarkable games in baseball history.

Three sluggers—Aaron, Mathews, and Joe Adcock—formed the heart of the Braves' lineup; together they would drill 110 homers and drive in 313 runs over the course of the season. Yet they could not reach base against Haddix. The 35-year-old southpaw used an assortment of change-ups, curveballs, fastballs, screwballs, and sliders to keep the Braves' big hitters off-balance inning after inning. "His control was perfect," Aaron said later. "In fact, he was perfect."

By the time Andy Pafko stepped up to the plate in the bottom of the ninth inning, Haddix had mowed down all 24 Milwaukee batters. Nothing, it seemed, was going to bother the Pittsburgh pitcher this night—not the severe head cold that had caused him to spend the afternoon in bed, nor the steady drizzle that had begun to fall. In 1953, his rookie season, Haddix had tossed a no-hitter through eight innings, only to yield a single to the first batter in the ninth. Six years later, he was gunning for something even rarer than a no-hitter: a perfect game. Since the turn of the century, such a feat had been accomplished only five times.

Haddix began the ninth inning by fanning Pafko. Johnny Logan then flied out, and Burdette struck out. Incredibly, the Pittsburgh hurler had retired every hitter he had faced, but he was not credited with a victory because the Pirates had failed to score off Burdette.

An inning later, Haddix became the first pitcher to hurl a perfect game beyond nine frames when Aaron grounded out to end the 10th. And when Del Crandall concluded the 11th by flying out, Haddix claimed the record for the longest no-hit game ever. Then he extended his own mark by pitching another perfect inning in the 12th.

Haddix's flawless performance finally ended in the bottom of the 13th inning, when Felix Mantilla poked a bouncer toward third; Don Hoak fielded the ball cleanly but threw low to first, allowing Mantilla to get on base. With the heart of the lineup coming up and Milwaukee still without a hit, Mathews, on his way to leading the league in home runs, sacrificed Mantilla over to second. Haddix then intentionally walked Aaron and tried to get Adcock, the next batter, to ground into an inning-ending double play.

With the count at one ball and no strikes, Haddix threw what he later described as "my only bad pitch," a high slider, to Adcock. The Braves' first baseman lashed the ball to deep right-center field for Milwaukee's lone hit of the night, and Mantilla trotted home with the winning run. In the span of 2 hours and 54 minutes, Harvey Haddix had pitched perhaps the greatest game of all time—*and had lost.*

If the Braves viewed this victory as a signal that 1959 was destined to be their year, they were badly mistaken. The ballclub drifted through the first two months of the summer and failed to win half its games. "We could never perform at our best as a team," Aaron maintained, "until we were being criticized or unless we had our backs to the wall." The ballplayers found themselves in the latter position in September; they trailed the San Francisco Giants by 4 games with only 20 left to play. "It was win or no pennant," Aaron recalled.

The Milwaukee players decided to win. The club closed out its schedule by capturing 15 of its final 20 ballgames, with the last of these triumphs coming against the Philadelphia Phillies on September 26, the concluding day of the season. The victory put the Braves into a tie for first place with the Los Angeles Dodgers, who had also squeezed past the Giants in the standings. For only the third time in National League history, the pennant had to be decided by a playoff, a best-of-three-games affair slated to open the next day in Milwaukee.

The Braves were a confident bunch heading into the playoff. "We were sure—everybody in Milwaukee was sure—that we were the superior team," Aaron said. A glance at the National League leaders board backed up his claim. Burdette and Spahn had tied for the league lead in wins with 21. Mathews had won his second home run title with 46. And Aaron had led the circuit in hits with 223, in slugging with a .636 percentage, and had captured his second batting crown with a career-high .355 average. "I might have had a second shot at the Triple Crown," he said later, "except that a fan in Philadelphia threw a bottle at me around midseason and I twisted my ankle when I saw it whizzing by."

Rain delayed the start of the first playoff game for nearly an hour. The Braves soon found themselves wishing the action had not begun at all. Los Angeles jumped out to an early one-run lead, spotted Milwaukee two runs in the bottom of the first inning, then came back, on the strength of catcher John Roseboro's sixth-inning home run, to win the contest, 3–2.

The ballgame proved doubly upsetting to the home team because of the poor turnout at the ballpark. Only 18,297 people braved the miserable weather and entered the 40,000-seat stadium. Apparently, the avid Milwaukee rooters had been spoiled by their ballclub's recent string of successes and were simply waiting for the World Series to begin. "I can't really blame them for that," Aaron said later, "because in a way, we took ourselves for granted."

The Braves flew to Los Angeles that same evening and seemed to bounce back the following afternoon at the Coliseum. Almost everyone in the lineup had a hand in building a 5–2 lead against Don Drysdale, the Dodgers starting pitcher. Meanwhile, Burdette appeared to be in absolute command of the Los Angeles batters. By the time the Braves hurler took the mound in the bottom of the ninth inning, he had retired the last 17 Dodgers to come to the plate. "We looked truly superior, like the superior team we were," Aaron recalled.

Burdette, however, gave up three straight singles; reliever Don McMahon was greeted by a two-run single that put Los Angeles within a run of Milwaukee, 5–4; then Carl Furillo evened the contest by hitting a sacrifice fly against Spahn, who had been brought in to pitch on only two days' rest. The game lasted three more innings, until the Braves lost it on an error by Mantilla in the bottom of the 12th. With the defeat, the team's shot at a third straight World Series appearance vanished.

"We should have won four pennants in a row," Aaron insisted. Instead, neither he nor the Milwaukee Braves ever played in a World Series again. ◆

9

"HOME RUN DERBY"

❦

T HE TELEVISION SHOW "Home Run Derby" was introduced to the American public in the fall of 1959. Each week, this half-hour program showcased two big league ballplayers competing head to head in a home-run-hitting contest held at the Los Angeles Dodgers' ballpark, the Coliseum. Any ball that landed in fair territory but did not leave the stadium counted as an out, and the player who hit the most balls over the fence in nine innings was declared the winner. He was also awarded a substantial amount of prize money and was invited back for the next show.

Henry Aaron was among the first major leaguers to appear on "Home Run Derby." Initially, he did not give himself much of a shot at performing well. "I wasn't accustomed to swinging for home runs," he explained. But if that was the case, then Aaron adapted to the competition in remarkable fashion, for he clouted more homers than any other contestant in 1959. The National League's two-time batting champ received $30,000 for his efforts, nearly as much as his annual salary with the Milwaukee Braves.

Aaron makes a supreme effort to catch a fly ball against the right-field wall in Philadelphia's Connie Mack Stadium on May 12, 1963. A superb defensive outfielder, he earned a Gold Glove in three of the first four years that the award was handed out.

"There's no doubt that he made me a better player," Aaron said of the slugging third baseman Eddie Mathews, a teammate for 13 years. At bat, the two ballplayers made for an especially dynamic duo, combining for more home runs than any other pair of team-mates in baseball history.

The prize money encouraged Aaron to rethink his approach to hitting. He had always taken great pride in being an all-around player and believed he had successfully avoided "being seduced by the money and glamour of home runs." After his appearance on "Home Run Derby," however, the outfielder slowly began to change his batting style. "No longer the skinny kid who was," he remembered, "all wrists and forearms," he sought to pull the ball more often to the left side of the diamond rather than drive it to the opposite field. "I noticed," he said wryly, "that they never had a show called 'Singles Derby.'"

According to his teammates, Aaron sought to hit more homers in part so he could keep pace with the ballclub's other star slugger, Eddie Mathews. "As the years went on, I thought he started competing with Mathews for home runs," Bill Bruton said. "I thought it was a personal thing." Mathews agreed: "Henry and I had a friendly rivalry. He pushed me and I pushed him. He'd win the home run title one year, I might win it the next. Rivalries were important to us."

Aaron could hardly have picked a better rival. The only ballplayer ever to clout 25 or more homers in each of his first 11 seasons, Mathews wound up his career as one of the top home run hitters in baseball history. When the left-handed-hitting third baseman hung up his spikes for good in 1968, his 512 lifetime home runs temporarily placed him sixth on the all-time list, behind only Babe Ruth (714), Willie Mays (587), Mickey Mantle (536), Jimmy Foxx (534), and Ted Williams (521).

Aaron and Mathews's private competition proved to be a long and healthy rivalry for the Braves. Working in tandem year after year, the two players set the National League record for most home runs by two teammates, breaking Gil Hodges and Duke Snider's old mark of 745 on May 2, 1965. By then, Aaron had almost drawn even with Mathews in their competition: Aaron had swatted 368 homers, only 10 less than Mathews did during that same 11-year span.

On August 20, exactly three and a half months after breaking the National League record, Aaron homered to tie the all-time big league mark for teammates that Lou Gehrig and Babe Ruth had established with the New York Yankees. The Braves' duo had to wait only three more days before they surpassed the two Yankees' 31-year-old record of 793. It was another two years before Aaron and Mathews's partnership came to an end; when it finally did, they had combined for 863 home runs.

As much as Aaron enjoyed teaming up with Mathews, there was one Braves player whom the slugging right fielder enjoyed joining forces with even more: his younger brother Tommie. According to Henry, Tommie was "an outstanding minor league hitter," and Milwaukee promoted him to the major leagues in 1962 after four seasons in their farm system. Four and a half years Henry's junior, Tommie became his brother's roommate on road trips and lived in Mequon with Henry and his wife, Barbara, and their four children—their daughter Dorinda had also

Tommie Aaron (right) lumbers up with his older brother Henry at the Milwaukee Braves' 1962 spring training camp in Bradenton. The two Aarons became teammates and roommates that season and played together in the major leagues for seven years.

arrived in 1962—whenever the Braves were in town. "We were a couple of proud Aarons in those days," Henry recalled.

Tommie, however, was not quite the ballplayer his brother was. The younger Aaron batted only .231 with eight home runs in his first season with Milwaukee. One of those homers occurred in Cincinnati in the same game that Henry hit one, a feat the brothers accomplished on two subsequent occasions.

In the years that followed, Tommie's home runs remained few and far between. Although he lasted in the majors for seven seasons—all of them with the Braves—he connected for only 13 home runs to accompany a lowly .229 lifetime batting average. Tommie was a versatile athlete who could play both the infield and the outfield. But as a slugger, he failed to fill the shoes of Joe Adcock, whom he had been groomed to replace. Henry accepted part of the blame. "With me around," he said, "it was difficult for Tommie to be his own ballplayer."

Henry did indeed cast a huge shadow, even when he failed to top the .300 mark he coveted. In 1960, he led the National League in runs batted in, fell one shy of the home run crown, and added a new wrinkle to his game: base-stealing, doubling his previous career high of eight. (He then averaged 22 stolen bases in each of the next eight seasons.) Yet Aaron's disappointment over batting a subpar .292 prompted a Milwaukee sportswriter to observe: "Henry Aaron is the only player in baseball who can hit 40 home runs and drive in 126 runs and consider it a bad year."

The following season, the 27-year-old boosted his batting average all the way back up to .327, launched 34 homers, and knocked in 120 runs. In 1962, he hit .323, raised his home run total to 45, and drove home another 128 runs. He posted similar numbers in 1963, and this time they nearly earned him the Triple Crown. Aaron's 44 home runs and 130 runs batted in topped the circuit, while his .319 batting average trailed league leader Tommy Davis's by a mere seven points.

Aaron also barely missed winning the batting title in each of the next two seasons. He finished third in 1964 with a .328 average and placed second in 1965 with a .318 mark. Roberto Clemente, the Pittsburgh Pirates' right fielder, hit 11 points higher than Aaron each of those years and won both crowns.

"I was young and at the peak of my career," Aaron recalled. "I was hitting. I was healthy. I was pulling my part of the load." But he did not have enough help. After the Braves' collapse in the 1958 World Series and their disastrous playoff the following year, the Milwaukee front office had decided to recast its team one by one.

The first person to depart the club was the manager, Fred Haney, who resigned a week after the 1959 playoffs. "There was still enough of the old team left to finish second to the Pirates in 1960," Aaron noted. But they did not stay around for long. Bill Bruton and Red Schoendienst moved on after the 1960 season. Wes Covington was waived, and Johnny Logan was shipped off in mid-1961. Felix Mantilla was claimed by the newly formed New York Mets in the 1961 expansion draft that also gave birth to the Houston Colt .45s (later renamed the Astros). Bob Buhl was sent packing in early 1962. Joe Adcock was traded in late 1962, Lew Burdette in mid-1963, and Del Crandall at the end of 1963.

"Faces seemed to change every week," Aaron remembered. "Players came and went like livestock." The managers did, too. Following Haney's departure, the Braves hired and then fired Charlie Dressen, Birdie Tebbetts, Bobby Bragan, Billy Hitchcock, and Luman Harris.

None of these field generals had as much talent to work with as Charlie Grimm and Fred Haney did. "The problem was," Aaron said, "that while the old Braves were being sent away, we weren't replacing them with good young players from our farm system." Only a handful of top-rank ballplayers arrived at Milwaukee County Stadium in the 1960s. The best of them were Joe Torre (1960); Tony Cloninger, Roy McMillan, and Mobile product Frank Bolling (1961); Denny Lemaster and Denis Menke (1962); Rico Carty (1963); and Felipe Alou (1964). "With the exception of Spahn, Mathews, and me," Aaron said, "we had become a team of kids."

The Braves' record tumbled as their veteran talent thinned out. Milwaukee finished in fourth place in 1961, fifth in 1962, sixth in 1963, and fifth in both 1964 and 1965. The team never compiled a worse record than 83–71 during that stretch. Yet its failure to win another pennant led to a sharp drop in attendance. So did the 1961 move of the Washington Senators to Minnesota, on Wisconsin's western border. Settling in the Minneapolis–St. Paul area

"We were a small group in a big league, and we understood that we had to stick to together," Aaron said of the bond that existed between himself, Roberto Clemente (left), Willie Mays (center), and the National League's other black and Hispanic stars. "Our names always seemed to run together in the league leaders, but we had a lot more in common than that."

and rechristening themselves the Twins, the former Senators gave baseball fans in the Midwest a new team to root for.

A misguided attempt by the Braves management to get the hometown fans to purchase beer at Milwaukee County Stadium served only to shrink attendance even further. Milwaukee's faithful followers loved to arrive early at the ballpark, gather around their ice chests filled with beer, and hold tailgate parties in the parking lot; it was an enthusiastic ritual that dated back to 1953 and the ballclub's arrival in a city that had been dubbed the brewery capital of the United States. Accordingly, when the Braves front office banned coolers from the ballpark and thereby forced the Milwaukee fans to buy beer at the stadium's concession stands, many of the team's supporters became enraged at being told they could not drink their own beer, and they stayed away from the ballgames in droves.

The falloff in attendance was startling. In 1957, when the Braves were at the height of their popularity, the team drew more than 2.2 million spec-

The end of a beautiful relationship: Aaron and Eddie Mathews take their farewell walk up the tunnel to the clubhouse following the Milwaukee Braves' final game at Milwaukee County Stadium. "It seemed unthinkable that it could happen in Milwaukee," Aaron said of the decision to move the ballclub to Atlanta after the 1965 season. "Not with those fans. Not with our team."

tators. That figure plummeted to 1.5 million in 1960 and dwindled to less than 770,000 in 1962. By then, it had become clear that the city of Milwaukee no longer considered the Braves its darlings.

The steady decline in attendance caused the ballclub to struggle financially, and in the summer of 1963 the first wave of rumors circulated that the franchise would be moving to another part of the country. The Southeast was reported to be the most likely choice. Boasting a large television market without any other big league teams in the area, it promised the Braves far more revenue than Milwaukee could ever offer.

Stories about the Braves relocating increased in the spring of 1964, when the city of Atlanta revealed its plans for the construction of a major league–size ballpark, Atlanta–Fulton County Stadium. The Braves' executives admitted later in the year that the team was indeed slated to head south to Atlanta. Immediately following this announcement, a legal battle ensued, and Milwaukee County obtained a court order to prevent the ballclub from moving until it had fulfilled its contract with Milwaukee County Stadium. The commitment for the Braves to remain in the city expired after the 1965 season.

"It was a terrible thing for it all to end that way," said Spahn, "because we had something special in Milwaukee. I tell you, any ballplayer missed something if he didn't play in Milwaukee during those 13 years." Spahn's career in Milwaukee concluded on an especially disappointing note: in November 1965, with little fanfare, the team's thrifty executives sold the high-priced southpaw to the last-place Mets.

Aaron said good-bye to Milwaukee in his own special way. On September 20, one week before the 1965 season ended, he belted his 398th career home run. It was the last home run ever hit by a Milwaukee Braves player in Milwaukee County Stadium. ❧

10

"I WAS TIRED OF BEING INVISIBLE"

Aaron blasts the 500th homer of his career on July 14, 1968, at Atlanta–Fulton County Stadium and becomes only the eighth player in baseball history to reach that mark. "I was strictly a guess hitter," he said, "which meant that I had to have a full knowledge of every pitcher I came up against and develop a strategy for hitting him. My method was to identify the pitches that a certain pitcher had and then eliminate all but one or two and wait for them. Usually, I would wait for his best pitch, because I knew he would use it sooner or later."

As SORRY AS Henry Aaron was to leave Wisconsin, he was not bidding farewell to a ballpark that had been a home run hitter's paradise. Aaron's output was proof that the ball did not carry exceptionally well at Milwaukee County Stadium. During his 12-year career with the Braves in Milwaukee, he hit more homers on the road (213) than he did at home (185).

It was not quite the same story down south. "The first time I took batting practice in Atlanta–Fulton County Stadium, I knew that my career was headed in a new direction," Aaron said. "Atlanta was the highest city in the major leagues, as well as the hottest, and if you could get the ball into the air, there was a good chance that it wouldn't come down in the playing field. . . . I changed my batting style immediately."

Aaron arrived in Atlanta in 1966 with a .320 lifetime batting average, the highest among all active players. Almost as impressive, he blasted the 400th home run of his career on April 20, a Ruthian shot that landed on the roof of Connie Mack Stadium. He thus became only the 11th player in baseball history to reach the 400 mark.

Aaron kept on crashing home runs during the rest of the campaign, and by the season's end he was the National League's top home run hitter (44) for the third time in his career. He also won his fourth runs-batted-in crown (127). Following his example, the Atlanta Braves scored more runs than any team in the league. The pitching staff, however, failed to keep pace with the hitters, and the ballclub finished the year in fifth place, 10 games behind three-time Cy Young Award–winner Sandy Koufax and the pitching-rich Los Angeles Dodgers.

Most postseasons, Aaron made public appearances on the Braves' behalf to help boost ticket sales. In the autumn of 1966, his personal appearances took him much farther afield than usual. That October, he embarked on a 17-day visit with U.S. military troops stationed in Vietnam. Joining him on the goodwill tour were his friend Stan Musial, teammate Joe Torre, American League all-stars Harmon Killebrew and Brooks Robinson, and famed baseball announcer Mel Allen.

The travelers followed up their trip to Southeast Asia with a visit to the White House, where they were greeted by President Lyndon B. Johnson. Being received by the president, Aaron said, "made me feel like I was finally in tall cotton, which was soon to get taller: A few months later, I signed my first $100,000 contract." Only five other ballplayers were earning as much: Koufax, Don Drysdale, Mickey Mantle, Willie Mays, and the American League's latest Triple Crown winner, Frank Robinson.

While the Braves were busy rewarding Aaron for his outstanding first season in Atlanta, the ballclub took a completely different tack with Eddie Mathews. Hitting half as many home runs (16) in 1966 as he did the previous year, the third baseman was shipped to the Houston Astros on New Year's Eve for two journeyman players and a minor leaguer to be named

A quintet of Mobile natives— (from left to right) Tommie Agee, Tommie Aaron, Cleon Jones, Henry Aaron, and Amos Otis— hold a reunion at Shea Stadium prior to a ballgame on May 14, 1969, between the Atlanta Braves and the New York Mets. Aaron later made his final postseason appearance when the two teams faced each other in the National League Championship Series.

later. Aaron learned that Paul Richards, the Braves' new general manager, had not even bothered to inform Mathews he had been traded.

The manner in which the player who had once been the cornerstone of the franchise was treated left Aaron stunned. Mathews, he noted, "was the only Brave to play in Boston, Milwaukee, and Atlanta. As far as I was concerned, he was Mr. Brave . . . a ballplayer's ballplayer [who] would do anything to win."

Without Mathews on the roster, Aaron represented the ballclub's last link with the great Milwaukee teams of the past—a fact he found hard to swallow. Even more difficult to accept was the kind of team the Braves had become: a floundering ballclub that lacked the kind of tough competitors Mathews, Lew Burdette, and Warren Spahn were. From them, Aaron had learned to play through pain and injuries, to always go hard for the team. But when he now looked at the word spelled out across the front of his home uniform, he was not fully convinced he was a member of the Braves.

Playing baseball in Atlanta only fueled Aaron's growing reservations about being a part of the ballclub. The hometown of civil rights leader Martin Luther King, Jr., Atlanta billed itself as the capital of the New South. Yet the racism that Aaron encountered in the Georgia city was centuries old and strongly reminded him of his days in the Sally League. "There was often a hate letter or two in the mail," he said, "and I was always concerned about Barbara and the kids being abused when they went to the ballpark. . . . Returning to the South took some of the boy from Mobile out of me, and replaced it with a man who was weary of the way things were. I was tired of being invisible."

Responding the best way he knew how, Aaron made his presence felt at the ballpark. In the clubhouse, he took the Braves' young black players under his wing the same way Bill Bruton had fended for him when he first broke into the majors. On the diamond, he continued to terrorize opposing pitchers. In 1967, he won his fourth home run title and barely missed being the runs-batted-in leader.

Aaron reached yet another milestone on July 14, 1968, when he hit his 500th career home run. That same summer, he was briefly united with another Mobile ballplayer, Satchel Paige, when the Braves activated the former Negro leagues star so he could qualify for a major league pension. Aaron was given the honor of squiring the 62-year-old Paige around the ballpark.

In baseball terms, Aaron was no longer a youngster, either. Entering the 1969 season, he was at an age, 35, when most players had already retired. Yet there was still plenty to keep him going. For one thing, he was just 208 hits short of 3,000 for his career, which was the one goal he had set for himself when he first entered the majors. Only eight other players had ever reached that mark—Cap Anson, Ty Cobb, Eddie Collins, Napoleon Lajoie, Stan Musial, Tris Speaker, Honus Wagner, and Paul Waner—and none of them had hit as many as 500 home runs. "To somebody like me," Aaron said, "having come along in a period when black players were only beginning to assume their rightful place in baseball—the chance to make history sounded like something worth pursuing with all my resources."

It would take Aaron until May 17, 1970, to collect his 3,000th career base hit. In the meantime, he passed another noteworthy milestone. On July 30, 1969—10 days after U.S. astronauts Neil Armstrong and Buzz Aldrin became the first men to land on the moon—he launched a rocket of his own: home run number 537. The blast put Aaron into third place on the all-time home run list, ahead of Mickey Mantle and trailing only Babe Ruth and Willie Mays.

In 1969, Mays hit only 13 homers and was showing signs of slowing down. Aaron, however, seemed to be getting stronger with age. He batted .300 for the season and, for the fourth time in his career, the number of homers he belted matched the 44 on his uniform. Best of all, his teammates Orlando Cepeda and Phil Niekro helped him carry the Braves into postseason play. Compiling a record of 93–69, Atlanta captured the National League's newly formed Western Division and earned the right to square off against the Eastern Division champs, the New York Mets, for the National League flag.

Led by Tom Seaver, the league's 1969 Cy Young Award winner, New York was in the process of completing a highly improbable season. The Las Vegas oddsmakers had established the Mets, who had finished no better than ninth in each of their first seven campaigns, as 100-to-1 longshots to win the pennant. Relying on superior pitching and timely hitting, New York had confounded the experts and had climbed all the way to first place in the National League East with a 100–62 record.

In the best-of-five-games league championship series against the Braves, the Mets' fabled starting pitching faltered. But their hitters picked up the slack, as did relievers Tug McGraw, Nolan Ryan, and

Aaron holds up the ball he stroked for his 3,000th base hit, at Cincinnati's Crosley Field on May 17, 1970, as Stan Musial (left), at the time the only other living person to have reached the milestone, and Atlanta Braves owner Bill Bartholomay (right) help him savor the moment. Musial's presence made the afternoon especially sweet for Aaron, who called Musial "one of my favorite ballplayers. . . . He treated everybody the same—black or white, superstar or scrub."

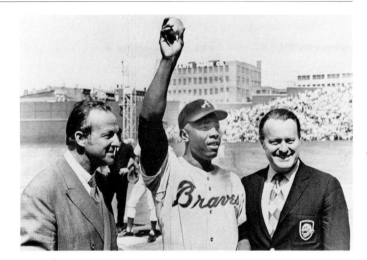

Ron Taylor, and New York swept Atlanta 9–5, 11–6, and 7–4. For Aaron, who batted .357, drove in seven runs, and homered in each contest, the 1969 National League Championship Series was the closest he would ever come to appearing in another World Series.

One disappointment soon followed another. In 1970, Barbara Aaron filed for a divorce. Her husband had admittedly been feeling out of sorts ever since the team had moved to Atlanta, and that sour mood had spread to his home life. The divorce was finalized the following February, whereupon Aaron moved into an apartment complex in downtown Atlanta; happily for him, he was still close enough to his four children that he could visit them whenever the Braves were in town.

In 1970, the Braves' record had dropped to 76–86, their first losing season since leaving Boston. The following year, with the ballclub once again settling into the middle of the standings, Aaron began to focus on surpassing Willie Mays as the National League's career home run leader. The Atlanta slugger had entered 1971 with 592 career home runs, just 36 behind Mays's total output.

The 40-year-old Giants star hit 18 homers in 1971, his 20th campaign, dipping below the 20-homer mark for the second time in three years. Aaron, playing in his 17th major league season, was slowing down a bit, too. He had injured his knee sliding into home plate the previous season, and it was still bothering him in 1971. He managed to rest his leg somewhat by shifting to first base and playing more games in the infield (71) than the outfield (60) for the first time in his big league career.

A switch in fielding positions had never affected Aaron's hitting abilities in the past, and it certainly did not bother him in 1971. On April 27, he hit his eighth homer of the season—and the 600th of his career. As the year wore on, he drove the ball out of the park at a faster clip than ever before. Coming up to bat less than 500 times, he closed out the campaign with 47 homers, his highest total ever. Always the complete player, he also posted a .327 batting average and batted in 118 runs.

The proof was there for everyone to see: at age 37, Aaron was hitting the ball as solidly as anyone. "I always told myself that my time would come," he said. And now it finally seemed close at hand.

Ever since the day Aaron made his National League debut, he had found himself in Willie Mays's shadow. He had heard for years that Mays was the league's best ballplayer and the only person who stood a chance of breaking Babe Ruth's all-time mark for home runs. Yet 1971 saw the gap between Aaron and Mays narrow to just seven home runs, with Mays rapidly approaching retirement. Meanwhile, Aaron was still going strong.

The Braves slugger took a look at his and Mays's statistics and saw a second chase taking shape. "I began to think for the first time," Aaron said, "that I had a shot at Ruth's record."

11

"THE MOST FABULOUS MOMENT IN THE WORLD"

❦

GREATEST DRAWING CARD IN HISTORY OF BASEBALL. HOLDER OF MANY HOME RUN AND OTHER BATTING RECORDS. GATHERED 714 HOME RUNS IN ADDITION TO FIFTEEN IN WORLD SERIES. So reads the plaque honoring Babe Ruth at the National Baseball Hall of Fame in Cooperstown, New York.

After making his American League debut in 1914 as a 19-year-old pitcher for the Boston Red Sox, Ruth established himself as the game's premier left-handed hurler by posting 65 victories in his first three full seasons. By then, a large number of baseball fans had grown weary of the low-scoring ballgames that characterized the sport's dead-ball era and were more interested in seeing the well-muscled Ruth bat than pitch. Eager to increase attendance, the Red Sox decided in 1918 to let their star southpaw split his playing time between the mound and the outfield. He responded with a .300 batting average and a share of the league lead in home runs with 11.

Aaron's Atlanta Braves teammates rush to embrace him as he steps on home plate to tie Babe Ruth's all-time home run record on April 4, 1974, at Cincinnati's Riverfront Stadium. "I just wanted to find home plate somewhere in the middle of the mob that was waiting there," Aaron remembered, "because when I did, the long, excruciating chase would at last be over. I still had one more home run to go to set the record, but for the first time in several long years, I wasn't chasing anybody."

The next year, Boston started Ruth in the outfield 111 times and asked him to pitch in only 17 games. Able to concentrate more fully on his hitting, he batted .322, drove in 114 runs, and became the first player in 19 years of American League play to top the 20-homer mark; his 29 round-trippers nearly doubled the old record of 16 set by Ralph Seybold 17 years earlier. Ruth's feat was so extraordinary that few fans believed he would ever hit that many homers again.

Beer baron Jacob Ruppert, owner of the New York Yankees, was not among the skeptics. On January 6, 1920, he purchased Ruth from Boston for $125,000, a king's ransom in those days. The Babe, as the left-handed slugger had been called ever since his rookie year with the Red Sox, immediately repaid Ruppert's faith in him. Playing a full season in the outfield, he astounded the baseball world by swatting 54 homers, more than any other *ballclub* in the league. Ruth clouted another 59 home runs the following season, then continued his long-ball barrage for a decade and a half. He wound up averaging a homer every 11.8 at-bats over the course of his 22-year career, the most productive rate in baseball history.

Amply rewarded for his phenomenal success, Ruth became the first professional athlete to earn a higher annual salary than the president of the United States. ("I had a better year," the ballplayer observed.) Day after day, the Babe acted like a youngster given piles of money and then turned loose in a toy store. He lived extravagantly and spread good cheer wherever he went, adding one wildly colorful story after another to his growing legend. He was a sportswriter's dream come true, and the public reveled in the accounts of the charismatic Ruth's larger-than-life antics. To them, he represented not only a new brand of baseball; he also personified the way Americans liked to view themselves: as brash and amiable upstarts.

Henry Aaron was nothing at all like Babe Ruth. The Bronx Bomber was a big spender who painted the town red every chance he got; Hammerin' Hank preferred to spend quiet evenings at home with his family or in his hotel room, dining on room-service food. The Babe swaggered; Henry took pains never to show anyone up. Clearly a loudmouth and a glutton, Ruth was hardly anyone's ideal role model; Aaron always carried himself like a gentleman. Yet the Braves slugger labored continually in the shadow of Willie Mays and Mickey Mantle, whereas the Yankees' Sultan of Swat was treated like royalty wherever he went.

To look at each man was to size him up immediately. Ruth, with a face as round as a full moon and dark wavy hair, had a body shaped like a beer barrel; Aaron, from head to toe, appeared as sleek and purposeful as a torpedo. Still, what many people chose to notice most about the two ballplayers was that Ruth was white and Aaron was black.

Whereas Babe Ruth was treated like royalty for becoming the all-time home run king, Aaron was subjected to insults and death threats as he closed in on the Sultan of Swat's crown. "There were times during the chase," Aaron recalled, "when I was so angry and tired and sick of it all that I wished I could get on a plane and not get off until I was some place where they never heard of Babe Ruth."

Dear Nigger,
Everybody loved Babe Ruth. You will be the most hated man
in this country if you break his career home run record.

Dear Mr. Nigger,
I hope you don't break the Babe's record. How do I tell my
kids that a nigger did it?

Dear Jungle Bunny,
You have the nerve to try to break the Babe's record. 1st
of all you're black so you have no business even being here.
. . . Personally I like you because I don't think your prejudice
like them bigots but cause your black you're an un-equal
to me.

The U.S. postal service delivered thousands of
these malicious letters to Aaron as he zeroed in on
Ruth's celebrated home run mark. With the hate mail
pouring in, the Braves' elder statesman turned for
support to Billye Williams, co-hostess of "Today
in Georgia," a local television talk show. Aaron
had gotten to know the recently widowed Williams
during the making of "Billye at the Bat," a series of
profiles on the Braves players, and their friendship
ripened in the months that followed. "She helped
bring me into the world of books and ideas and made
me more conversant in the things I believed in,"
Aaron said of the former English teacher at Morris
Brown College. "At the same time, I made her a
baseball fan."

It did not take much prodding for Williams—
or her six-year-old daughter, Ceci—to appreciate
Aaron's handiwork at the ballpark. On May 31, 1972,
he socked his 648th homer to draw even with Willie
Mays for second place on the all-time list; he then
hit 11 home runs over the next two months to move
well past Mays and within a season or two of catching
Ruth. On August 6, the Braves' 38-year-old superstar—often called Supe by his teammates—reached
another milestone: he blasted his 660th homer to

break Ruth's record for most home runs hit by a player with one team.

Homering at a faster rate than every other major leaguer for the second year in a row, Aaron drove 34 balls out of the park in 1972. Two of them came on September 2, when he surpassed Stan Musial's all-time total bases mark of 6,134. "If there is any one record that I think best represents what I was all about as a hitter," Aaron said, "that's the one, because as far as I was concerned, the object of batting was to hit the ball and get as many bases as possible." Still, most baseball fans paid little attention to the records he was piling up. Only one mark seemed to count: Ruth's fabled 714 home runs.

And now, as Aaron headed into the 1973 season, he trailed Ruth by only 41 homers. "No player ever had as much to play for as I had that year," he recalled. "I was on the verge of doing something that would give me a place in baseball history, and I couldn't wait to do it."

Billye Williams watches her future husband zero in on the all-time home run mark near the end of the 1973 season. Escaping briefly from the spotlight of his record-breaking chase, Aaron flew with Williams to Jamaica and married her on November 12.

> Dear Hank Aaron,
> Retire or die! . . . You'll be in Montreal and St. Louis in August. You will die in one of those games. I'll shoot you in one of them.

> Mr. Aaron,
> If you do not retire from the baseball seen (QUIT) your family will inherit a great bit of trouble. We can't make this sound any clearer (DEATH).

The menacing letters arrived by the truckload in 1973, prompting the Braves front office to weave a web of security around Aaron. The Federal Bureau of Investigation (FBI) was called in to screen his mail and to look into the threatening phone calls being placed to his parents and children. Policeman Calvin Wardlaw was asked to escort the ballplayer to and from Atlanta–Fulton County Stadium. Meanwhile, a plot was unearthed to kidnap Aaron's oldest daughter, Gaile, and the FBI assigned several agents to shadow her at Fisk University, where she was a student.

> Dear Hank Aaron,
> I got orders to do a bad job on you if and when you get 10 from B. Ruth record. A guy in Atlanta and a few in Miami Fla don't seem to care if they have to take care of your family too.

> Dear Hank Aaron,
> I hate you!!!! Your such a little creap! I hate you and your family. I'D LIKE TO KILL YOU!! BANG BANG YOUR DEAD. P.S. It mite happen.

Anytime the FBI told Aaron about a death threat, he advised his teammates to keep their distance in the dugout in case someone actually did try to shoot him. During these tense times, it helped to have Eddie Mathews by his side. Aaron's good friend and former teammate had returned to Atlanta in mid-1972 as the Braves manager.

Along with the death threats, Aaron found himself smack in the middle of a media circus. Wherever he went, interviewers thrust microphones in front of his face and camera crews recorded his every move. Those few times when television correspondents, magazine reporters, and the foreign press were not besieging him with questions, autograph hounds stepped forward and demanded his signature. "It should have been the most enjoyable time in my life," bemoaned Aaron, "and instead it was hell."

A bit of relief came in May, when several sportswriters wrote articles about the stacks of hate mail being delivered to Aaron. As soon as these stories appeared in the newspapers, a flood of supportive messages began to pour in. All told, Aaron received 930,000 letters in 1973, far more than any other private citizen, said the U.S. Postal Service. The Braves assigned him a secretary to help answer the mail, but the Atlanta slugger saved his best response for the ballpark. There he embarked on a hitting spree, belting 27 home runs by the All-Star break, including number 700. He recalled, "There was something about getting [number 700] that made me feel I was almost at my destination, like I had been traveling the back roads for twenty years and suddenly I was on Ruth's street, turning into his driveway."

Even so, Aaron did not complete the journey in 1973. On the next-to-last day of the season, he moved within one of Ruth's mark, walloping a slow curveball for home run number 713. It was also his 40th round-tripper of the year and made the Braves the first team ever to have three players collect 40 home runs in a season. (Third baseman Darrell Evans and second baseman Davey Johnson shared the honor with Aaron.)

The following afternoon, almost 40,000 people arrived at Atlanta–Fulton County Stadium to see if Aaron could equal Ruth's record before the season ended. The Atlanta left fielder singled in his first three at-bats, pushing his batting average up to .300 for the 14th time in his big league career. He came to bat once more, in the bottom of the eighth inning, and popped out to second base, then trotted to the outfield for the final frame. As he did, the remaining fans stood and cheered, keeping up their applause for almost five minutes. It was the first heartfelt ovation Aaron had ever received in Atlanta.

With the home run chase on hold for the winter, Aaron tried to enjoy his celebrity status. After becoming the only active player to throw out the ceremonial first ball at a World Series, he peppered his offseason with banquet appearances and guest spots on television shows. On November 12, he took time out from his busy schedule to marry Billye

"I hit it squarely, although not well enough that I knew it was gone. The ball shot out on a line. . . ."

Williams in Jamaica and then relax on a nearby beach. But the ghost of Babe Ruth would not let Henry unwind completely. He still had a job to do.

Aaron went back to work in Cincinnati's Riverfront Stadium on Thursday, April 4, 1974, against Reds pitcher Jack Billingham. Batting in the top of the first inning, the Atlanta slugger let three balls and a strike sail by before Billingham threw the pitch Aaron had been waiting for: a sinker in the strike zone. Swinging for the first time that season, he deposited the ball in the left-center-field seats. "It was like I had landed on the moon," he remembered of the record-tying home run. "I was there. All I had to do now was take the next step."

Atlanta did not play the following day, and the Braves' top brass kept Aaron out of the lineup on Saturday because they wanted him to break the all-time record when the team returned to Atlanta on Monday. Declaring that sitting Aaron on the bench jeopardized the sport's integrity, the commissioner of baseball, Bowie Kuhn, insisted that Aaron play in Cincinnati on Sunday. He did, striking out two times against Clay Kirby before Mathews removed him in the seventh inning in favor of Ralph Garr.

The Braves held their season opener the following evening, April 8, against the Los Angeles Dodgers. Rain fell intermittently on the 53,775 fans who had arrived at Atlanta–Fulton County Stadium to witness baseball history in the making. Among those present were some of the key figures in Aaron's past: his parents; Ed Scott; John Mullen; Charlie Grimm; and Donald Davidson, the Braves' traveling secretary and one of Aaron's closest friends. They were chauffeured onto the field and took their places at Mobile, Indianapolis, Milwaukee, Bradenton, and Atlanta on a red-white-and-blue map of the United States painted on the center-field grass. "It seemed like the only people not there were the President of the United States and the commissioner of baseball," Aaron later said of the crowd, the biggest in team history.

Herbert and Estella Aaron jump for joy as their son Henry hits the ball out of Atlanta–Fulton County Stadium.

The pregame ceremonies included balloons and cannons and performances by a drill team, a band, a choir, and a war dance on the pitcher's mound by Chief Nok-A-Homa, the club's mascot, who then scurried off to his tipi in the left-field corner. Herbert Aaron, Sr., capped off the festivities by throwing out the first ball. "I just hope I can get this thing over with tonight—as soon as possible," his son said quietly in the dugout.

Aaron walked his first time up against veteran left-hander Al Downing without taking the bat off his shoulder. He came to the plate again in the fourth inning, with two outs and Darrell Evans on first base. Downing threw his initial offering in the dirt, which prompted home-plate umpire Satch Davidson to remove the ball from play and signal Frank Pulli, the first-base umpire, to toss the pitcher another baseball. Each ball used during Aaron's turn at bat was specially marked with invisible ink so it could be easily

The newly crowned home run king holds aloft the specially marked ball he drove over the left-center-field fence on April 8, 1974, to break Babe Ruth's all-time mark. Aaron said later, "If the home run record gives me more power to inspire children—and I know that it does—then the ordeal was worth every moment of sleep I lost and every hurt I felt from every hate letter."

identified if the Braves star should swat it into the stands.

Downing's next pitch was low and down the heart of the plate—just where Aaron was expecting it. He shifted his weight forward and ripped the baseball to deep left-center field, watching its flight as he bolted out of the batter's box.

"Fergie, that might be it," the home-plate umpire said to catcher Joe Ferguson.

Center-fielder Bill Buckner raced to the outfield fence and leaped for the ball, but it carried over his outstretched glove and into the Braves' bullpen. Reliever Tom House snared the baseball and immediately raised both arms in triumph, then came sprinting toward the infield with his prized possession. "Hammer, here it is!" he shouted among the crush of welcoming teammates who had mobbed Aaron the instant he touched home plate. Estella Aaron, who had climbed onto the field from her box seat, gave her son an even bigger hug than when he departed for the Mobile railroad depot to join the Indianapolis Clowns 22 years earlier. The raggedy kid who wore his sister Sarah's hand-me-down pants had grown up into a 40-year-old ballplayer who had just touched millions of lives.

More than 35 million television viewers and radio listeners, in fact, witnessed or heard the monumental blast the instant it happened. Among them were President Richard M. Nixon, who immediately placed a congratulatory phone call to Aaron, and 67-year-old Satchel Paige, watching the game with 17 relatives—"All these sisters-in-law of mine"—in Kansas City. One of the few fans who missed the moment was Bowie Kuhn, who had decided to stay away from the ballgame after ordering the Braves to play Aaron in Cincinnati. At the time of the home run, the commissioner of baseball was giving a speech to the Wahoo Club in Cleveland.

The smashing of Babe Ruth's all-time mark made front-page news around the world. A Japanese reporter began his account of Aaron's home run beneath the headline WHITE BALL DANCES THROUGH ATLANTA'S WHITE MIST: "In my Atlanta hotel room I now begin writing this copy. I know I have to be calm. But I find it impossible to prevent my writing hand from continuing to shake." The sports correspondent for *El Sol de Mexico* was just as awestruck: "We lived through this historic moment, the most fabulous in the world. Thanks to God we witnessed this moment of history."

But the most telling comment of all came as Aaron walked to the on-deck circle for his next at-bat. "Come on, Supe," said Ralph Garr, "break Hank Aaron's record." ⚾

12

"BASEBALL COUNTS"

Henry Aaron's world was turned upside down by home run number 715. "I was the Home Run King," he realized. "For better or for worse, I had to learn to live with that, because it would be that way for the rest of my life."

The benefits of breaking Babe Ruth's record enabled Aaron to meet many political leaders, professional athletes, and Hollywood stars. It won him invitations to state dinners at the White House and the opportunity to address Congress. But he did not take long to discover "there was also a dark side to being the Home Run King, that being the complete surrender of a normal and private life."

At the same time, Aaron grew more disenchanted than ever with the people of Atlanta. What happened on April 10, 1974, seemed typical of the city: two days after he toppled Ruth's record, only 6,500 Braves fans attended the Wednesday game. As the season wore on, he let the ballclub know that 1974 would mark his last campaign in the South.

Aaron returns to Milwaukee in 1975 to finish up his playing career with the Brewers. "I'll never forget," he said, "walking out on that County Stadium field, the same field my teammates had carried me off when we won the pennant in 1957, and hearing those fans screaming and singing for me. It made me realize how much I'd missed that place."

Fifty thousand people at Tokyo's Korakuen Stadium watch Aaron duel Sadaharu Oh (opposite page), Japanese baseball's all-time home run champion, in a home run–hitting contest on November 1, 1974. "Oh was much more of a national hero in Japan than I was in America," Aaron said. "In fact, I was more of a hero in Japan than I was in America."

Aaron's final summer with Atlanta was filled with good-byes. The ballclub saluted him in July with another Henry Aaron Day, and this tribute was followed by farewell ceremonies at every National League ballpark. "The most memorable occasion," he recalled, "was in New York, when I met the local dignitaries at City Hall—including Mrs. Babe Ruth and Mrs. Lou Gehrig—then rode in a motorcade through Harlem and spoke to a crowd of about 5,000 people at a city park. When I saw all those black faces staring up at me, I remembered being part of the Davis Avenue crowd staring up at Jackie Robinson when he came to Mobile."

Aaron relished that role, and he still enjoyed playing baseball too, even though his skills had

started to slip. Batting only 340 times in 1974, he finished the season with a .268 average and 20 home runs, half as many as he had hit the previous year. His totals were still respectable enough to convince him to continue playing. But if he harbored any thoughts of returning to Atlanta, they were squelched when only 11,000 fans showed up for what was billed as his final game in a Braves uniform.

The following month, Aaron demonstrated that he still possessed considerable drawing power. When he arrived in Tokyo on November 1 to compete in a home run–hitting contest with Sadaharu Oh, Japanese baseball's perennial long-ball champion, more than 2,000 reporters were waiting at the airport to greet Aaron. Another 50,000 rooters arrived at

Korakuen Stadium to watch the international version of "Home Run Derby." Upholding his honor, the American baseball star defeated his Oriental counterpart in the contest, 10 home runs to 9.

Later that night, Bud Selig, owner of the Milwaukee Brewers, woke Aaron with a phone call. The veteran ballplayer must have thought he was dreaming when Selig told him he had just been traded to the four-year-old Milwaukee franchise in exchange for outfielder Dave May and minor league pitcher Roger Alexander. The trade had a downside: Aaron would have to bat against pitchers with whom he was not familiar, for the Brewers, unlike the Braves, played in the American League. Nevertheless, Aaron was overjoyed by Selig's news. "I still loved Milwaukee," he said, "and unlike Atlanta, Milwaukee still loved me."

The Cream City did indeed. Almost 48,000 rabid fans showed up at the Brewers' chilly home opener in 1975, serenading the long-absent star with the popular strains of "Hello, Dolly." "Hello, Henry," they crooned. "It's so nice to have you back where you belong."

Playing primarily as a designated hitter, the 41-year-old was hardly the Hammerin' Hank of days gone by. On May 1, he went four-for-four and broke Babe Ruth's all-time record of 2,211 runs batted in. Aaron, however, did not experience many other shining moments in his second tour at Milwaukee County Stadium. He hit only .234 with 12 home runs in 1975, and he failed to improve on those numbers midway through the next year. That was when he decided to retire after the 1976 season.

Aaron socked the last home run of his career—number 755—on July 20 against the California Angels. He concluded his 23 years as a big leaguer two months later, playing in his 3,298th game and going to bat for the 12,364th time; both figures were then the most in baseball history. He singled in his last plate appearance for base hit number 3,771, finishing second only to Ty Cobb in that category, and wound up tied with Ruth for second in runs scored with 2,174, trailing Cobb by just 71. Equally impressive, Aaron's lifetime batting mark stood at .305, and he averaged 33 homers and 100 runs batted in per year.

As soon as the 1976 season ended, Aaron announced that he was taking a job with the Braves. Media mogul Ted Turner had purchased the franchise that spring, and one of the first moves he had made as the new owner was to invite Aaron back to the ballclub as player development director. The home run king thought the position was ideal because it required him to oversee the organization's farm system and carried with it a large amount of responsibility. After years of battling for black advancement, he would have rejected any post in which he was merely a figurehead.

Aaron soon became baseball's highest-ranking black executive, and he spoke pointedly about racial progress when he was inducted into the Baseball Hall of Fame in August 1982. "I'm proud to be standing," he said during the ceremony at Cooperstown, "where Jackie Robinson, Roy Campanella, and others made it possible for players like Frank Robinson and myself to prove that a man's ability is limited only by his lack of opportunity."

Continuing to lead the way by example, Aaron was promoted by the Braves in 1990 to senior vice-president and assistant to the president. Atlanta won the National League pennant the following year by relying heavily on Steve Avery, David Justice, and several other young players whom Aaron had helped develop in the organization's farm system. Sadly, he received almost no credit for assembling a champion-

Aaron chats with Ernie Banks during a ceremony at Atlanta–Fulton County Stadium on June 5, 1989, to honor the living legends of Negro baseball. Aaron said later, "I feel it's my task to carry on where Jackie Robinson left off, and I only know of one way to go about it. It's the only way I've ever had of dealing with things like fastballs and bigotry— keep swinging at them."

ship team. According to former All-Star first baseman Bill White, who became the highest-ranking black executive in the sport when he ascended to the National League presidency in 1989, the lack of respect shown to Aaron perfectly illustrated the plight of blacks in baseball.

In a similar vein, the presidency of the National League has become a position Aaron refuses to hold, despite being well qualified for it. In mid-1992, when White was in his final year as league president, he stated that he had refrained from speaking out about racism in baseball because he feared the owners would retaliate by keeping other blacks from succeeding him. Aaron, who had been urged by his good friend White to seek the office, subsequently told the press, "I don't want to be confined. I don't want anybody to think that I'll go in and keep my mouth closed. So the job is not for me."

Aaron has chosen instead to broaden his range of activities. "In recent years," he noted, "I've served on committees for leukemia and cancer research and executive boards of PUSH [People United to Serve Humanity], the NAACP [the National Association for the Advancement of Colored People], and Big Brothers/Big Sisters. Through Big Brothers/Big Sisters and Arby's, I've been involved with a Hank Aaron Scholarship Program that has raised more than $5 million to send kids to college. I've also joined up with Sadaharu Oh in a program to develop baseball in Third World countries." And he is now a vice-president with the Cable News Network.

But baseball still remains the field in which Henry Aaron possesses the most clout. "And that's okay," says the Mobile marvel who took the baseball world by storm, "because people pay attention to baseball. Baseball counts. It counts a lot." ✺

HENRY "HANK" L. AARON
MILWAUKEE N.L., ATLANTA N.L.,
MILWAUKEE A.L., 1954-1976

HIT 755 HOME RUNS IN 23-YEAR CAREER TO
BECOME MAJORS' ALL-TIME HOMER KING. HAD
20 OR MORE FOR 20 CONSECUTIVE YEARS, AT
LEAST 30 IN 15 SEASONS AND 40 OR BETTER
EIGHT TIMES. ALSO SET RECORDS FOR GAMES
PLAYED (3,298), AT-BATS (12,364), LONG HITS
(1,477), TOTAL BASES (6,856), RUNS BATTED
IN (2,297). PACED N.L. IN BATTING TWICE
AND HOMERS, RUNS BATTED IN AND SLUGGING
PCT. FOUR TIMES EACH. WON MOST VALUABLE
PLAYER AWARD IN N.L. IN 1957.

APPENDIX:
CAREER STATISTICS

YEAR		G	AB	H	2B	3B	HR	R	RBI	BB	SO	SB	BA	SA	OBA
1954	MIL N	122	468	131	27	6	13	58	69	28	39	2	.280	.447	.321
1955		153	602	189	**37**	9	27	105	106	49	61	3	.314	.540	.366
1956		153	609	**200**	**34**	14	26	106	92	37	54	2	**.328**	.558	.367
1957		151	615	198	27	6	**44**	118	**132**	57	58	1	.322	.600	.380
1958		153	601	196	34	4	30	109	95	59	49	4	.326	.546	.386
1959		154	629	**223**	46	7	39	116	123	51	54	8	**.355**	**.636**	.403
1960		153	590	172	20	11	40	102	**126**	60	63	16	.292	.566	.357
1961		155	603	197	**39**	10	34	115	120	56	64	21	.327	.594	.384
1962		165	592	191	28	6	45	127	128	66	73	15	.323	.618	.391
1963		161	631	201	29	4	**44**	**121**	**130**	78	94	31	.319	**.586**	.394
1964		145	570	187	30	2	24	103	95	62	46	22	.328	.514	.394
1965		150	570	181	**40**	1	32	109	89	60	81	24	.318	.560	.383
1966	ATL N	158	603	168	23	1	**44**	117	**127**	76	96	21	.279	.539	.359
1967		155	600	184	37	3	**39**	**113**	109	63	97	17	.307	**.573**	.373
1968		160	606	174	33	4	29	84	86	64	62	28	.287	.498	.355
1969		147	547	164	30	3	44	100	97	87	47	9	.300	.607	.396
1970		150	516	154	26	1	38	103	118	74	63	9	.298	.574	.386
1971		139	495	162	22	3	47	95	118	71	58	1	.327	**.669**	.412
1972		129	449	119	10	0	34	75	77	92	55	4	.265	.514	.390
1973		120	392	118	12	1	40	84	96	68	51	1	.301	.643	.404
1974		112	340	91	16	0	20	47	69	39	29	1	.268	.491	.343
1975	MIL A	137	465	109	16	2	12	45	60	70	51	0	.234	.355	.335
1976		85	271	62	8	0	10	22	35	35	38	0	.229	.369	.317
23 YEARS		3,298	12,364	3,771	624	98	755	2,174	2,297	1,402	1,383	240	.305	.555	.376

NATIONAL LEAGUE CHAMPIONSHIP SERIES

YEAR		G	AB	H	2B	3B	HR	R	RBI	BB	SO	SB	BA	SA	OBA
1969	ATL N	3	14	5	2	0	3	3	7	0	1	0	.357	1.143	.357

WORLD SERIES

YEAR		G	AB	H	2B	3B	HR	R	RBI	BB	SO	SB	BA	SA	OBA
1957	MIL N	7	28	11	0	1	3	5	7	1	6	0	.393	.786	.414
1958		7	27	9	2	0	0	3	2	4	6	0	.333	.407	.419
		14	55	20	2	1	3	8	9	5	12	0	.364	.600	.417

(Numbers in **boldface** refer to league-leading totals.)

HENRY AARON'S RANKING AMONG THE LIFETIME BATTING LEADERS

Extra-base Hits	1,477	1st	Games	3,298	3rd
Home Runs	755	1st	Doubles	624	8th
Runs Batted In	2,297	1st	HR Frequency	16.4	12th
Total Bases	6,856	1st	Slugging Average	.555	12th
At-bats	12,364	2nd	Bases on Balls	1,402	19th
Runs	2,174	(Tie)2nd	Strikeouts	1,383	27th
Base Hits	3,771	3rd	Batting Average	.305	107th

CHRONOLOGY

─────── ⟨⟩ ───────

1934   Born Henry Aaron on February 5 in Mobile, Alabama

1942   Moves to nearby Toulminville

1948   Attends a public appearance by Jackie Robinson

1950   Joins the Mobile Black Bears

1951   Attends a Brooklyn Dodgers tryout camp

1952   Joins the Indianapolis Clowns; signed by Boston Braves scout Dewey Griggs on June 14; assigned by the Braves to the Eau Claire Bears of the Northern League; wins the Northern League's Rookie of the Year Award; helps the Clowns win the Negro League World Series; graduates from high school

1953   Assigned by the Milwaukee Braves to the Jacksonville Tars of the South Atlantic (Sally) League; helps integrate professional baseball in the Deep South; named the Sally League's most valuable player; marries Barbara Lucas on October 6; learns to play the outfield in the Puerto Rican League

1954   First daughter, Gaile, is born; Aaron gets first major league base hit on April 15 off Vic Raschi of the St. Louis Cardinals; hits first big league home run on April 12 off Raschi

1955   Makes first appearance in the All-Star Game; named the Braves' most valuable player; joins a touring all-star team of black major leaguers

1956   Wins first National League batting title

1957   First son, Hankie, is born; Aaron hits 100th career home run on August 15 off Don Gross of the Cincinnati Reds; wins first National League home run and runs-batted-in crowns; hits first World Series home run on October 5 off Bob Turley of the New York Yankees; the Braves win the World Series; Aaron named the National League's most valuable player; attends Henry Aaron Day in Mobile; sons Gary and Lary are born

1958   Aaron wins first Gold Glove Award; plays in his second World Series

1959   Wins second batting title; hits three homers in a game against the San Francisco Giants on June 21; appears on "Home Run Derby"

1960   Hits 200th career home run on July 3 off Ron Kline of the Cardinals; wins second runs-batted-in crown

1961   Aaron, Eddie Mathews, Joe Adcock, and Frank Thomas become the first four players ever to hit successive homers, in the seventh inning against the Reds on June 8

1962   Aaron's daughter Dorinda is born

1963   Aaron hits 300th career home run off Roger Craig of the New York Mets on April 19; wins second home run crown and third runs-batted-in title

1965   Hits last home run by a Milwaukee Braves player in Milwaukee County Stadium, on September 20

1966   Hits 400th career home run off Bob Priddy of the Giants on April 20; sets major league record with Eddie Mathews for most career home runs by teammates (863) on August 23; wins third home run crown and fourth runs-batted-in title; receives first invitation to visit the White House

1967   Wins fourth home run crown

1968   Hits 500th career home run off Mike McCormick of the Giants on July 14

1969   Moves into third place on the all-time home run list on July 30; hits three home runs in first and only National League Championship Series appearance

1970   Collects 3,000th career base hit on May 17

1971   Divorces Barbara Aaron; hits 600th career home run off Gaylord Perry of the Giants on April 27

1972   Moves into second place on the all-time home run list on June 10; sets all-time record for most home runs (660) hit by a player with one team, on August 6; sets all-time mark for most total bases (6,135), on September 2

1973   Hits 700th career home run off Ken Brett of the Philadelphia Phillies on July 21; joins Darrell Evans and Davey Johnson as the first trio of teammates to hit 40 or more homers in the same season; marries Billye Williams on November 12 and adopts her daughter, Ceci

1974   Ties Babe Ruth's all-time home run record (714) on April 4 against Jack Billingham of the Reds; hits career home run number 715 off Al Downing of the Los Angeles Dodgers on April 8 to become the all-time home run champion; plays last game for the Braves; traded to the Milwaukee Brewers on November 2 for Roger Alexander and Dave May

1975   Sets all-time runs-batted-in mark (2,212) on May 1

1976   Hits last home run of career (755) on July 20; becomes player development director of the Atlanta Braves

1982   Inducted into the Baseball Hall of Fame

1990   Becomes senior vice-president and assistant to the president of the Braves

FURTHER READING

———————— •◖◗• ————————

Aaron, Henry, with Furman Bisher. *"Aaron, r.f."* Cleveland: World Publishing Company, 1968.

Aaron, Henry, with Lonnie Wheeler. *I Had a Hammer: The Hank Aaron Story*. New York: HarperCollins, 1991.

Buege, Bob. *The Milwaukee Braves: A Baseball Eulogy*. Milwaukee: Douglas American Sports Publication, 1988.

Chadwick, Bruce. *When the Game Was Black and White: The Illustrated History of Baseball's Negro Leagues*. New York: Abbeville, 1993.

Dixon, Phil and Patrick J. Hannigan, Jr. *The Negro Leagues: A Photographic History*. Mattituck, NY: Amereon, 1992.

Hirshberg, Al. *Henry Aaron: Quiet Superstar*. New York: Putnam, 1969.

Holway John B. *Black Diamonds: Life in the Negro Leagues from the Men Who Lived It*. New York: Stadium Books, 1991.

———. *Blackball Stars: Negro League Pioneers*. New York: Carroll & Graf, 1992.

Peterson, Robert. *Only the Ball Was White: A History of Legendary Black Players and All-Black Professional Teams*. New York: Oxford University Press, 1992.

Plimpton, George. *One for the Record: The Inside Story of Hank Aaron's Chase for the Home-Run Record*. New York: Harper & Row, 1974.

Robinson, Jackie. *I Never Had It Made*. New York: Putnam, 1972.

Rogosin, Donn. *Invisible Men: Life in Baseball's Negro Leagues*. New York: Atheneum, 1983.

Scott, Richard. *Jackie Robinson*. New York: Chelsea House, 1987.

Tygiel, Julius. *Baseball's Great Experiment: Jackie Robinson and His Legacy*. New York: Oxford University Press, 1983.

INDEX

RICHARD SCOTT RENNERT is the author of two previous sports biographies, *Jackie Robinson* and *Jesse Owens*. He is also the editor of more than three dozen baseball books for children and adults. He loves to play the game, too, although he is not quite the home run threat that Henry Aaron was.

NATHAN IRVIN HUGGINS, one of America's leading scholars in the field of black studies, helped select the titles for the BLACK AMERICANS OF ACHIEVEMENT series, for which he also served as senior consulting editor. He was the W.E.B. Du Bois Professor of History and of Afro-American Studies at Harvard University and the director of the W.E.B. Du Bois Institute for Afro-American Research at Harvard. He received his doctorate from Harvard in 1962 and returned there as a professor in 1980 after teaching at Columbia University, the University of Massachusetts, Lake Forest College, and the California State University, Long Beach. He was the author of four books and dozens of articles, including *Black Odyssey: The Afro-American Ordeal in Slavery*, *The Harlem Renaissance*, and *Slave and Citizen: The Life of Frederick Douglass*, and was associated with the Children's Television Workshop, National Public Radio, the Boston Athenaeum, the Museum of Afro-American History, the Howard Thurman Educational Trust, and Upward Bound. Professor Huggins died in 1989, at the age of 62, in Cambridge, Massachusetts.

PICTURE CREDITS